WOMEN AND TERRORISM

Women and Terrorism

LUISELLA DE CATALDO NEUBURGER

and

TIZIANA VALENTINI

Translated into English by Leo Michael Hughes

Consultant Editor

Jo Campling

St. Martin's Press
New York

St. Martin's Press, Scholarly and Reference Division,
175 Fifth Avenue, New York, N.Y. 10010

First published in the United States of America in 1996

First published as *Il filo di Arianna,* CEDAM, Padua, 1992.

Printed in Great Britain

ISBN 0–312–12716–2

Library of Congress Cataloging-in-Publication Data
De Cataldo Neuburger, Luisella.
Women and terrorism / Luisella de Cataldo Neuburger and Tiziana
Valentini; translated into English by Leo Michael Hughes.
p.   cm.
Translated from the Italian.
Includes bibliographical references and index.
ISBN 0–312–12716–2 (cloth)
1. Women terrorists—History.   2. Terrorism—History.
I. Valentini, Tiziana.   II. Title.
HV6431.D36   1996
303. 6'25'082—dc20   95–13884
                                                                CIP

Contents

Prologue: Myth and Femininity

I am Isis, mistress of every land. I laid down laws for all, and ordained things no one may change. I divided the earth from heaven, made manifest the paths of the stars, prescribed the course of the sun and the moon . . . What I have made law can be dissolved by no man.

John Langdon-Davies, *A Short History of Women*

Hecate, high priestess of the goddess of fight, stands guard at the entrance to the underworld and the realm of the dead in secret identity with Persephone.

Medea, fascinatingly evil, offers such sinister sacrifices that the poet does not dare describe them. Betrayed, she does not hesitate to sacrifice her children so that their father Jason may also be struck and annihilated by ill fortune, as he deserves.

The Parcaes, who sever the thread of life.

The Gorgons, on whom neither sun nor moon ever shine, whose glance turns the beholder to stone.

The Erinyes, personalised projections of maternal ire, implacable ministers of vengence.

Pythia, *entheos, plena deo*, who prophesies in the first person in order to have the god within her.

The Sibyls, oracular voices who incarnate divine revelation.

Electra, inexorable in her dream of vengeance.

In sum, femininity as carrier of life and death, oracular voices, divine medium, ruthless instrument of vengeance, depository of 'strong' and immanent values, the point of intersection of pleasure and death, of sensuality and assassination.

Feminine figures have a dramatic voracity that saturates the imaginary and the real world. The very same voracity that still saturates the social world when women present themselves anew as bearers and interpreters of the ancient archetypal message. And inevitably they once again become Medea, Phaedra, Salome, Judith . . .

The woman who brandishes an automatic weapon incarnates the definitive and irrevocable power of her mysterious myth, of her life and death rites, just as the Gorgon turns men into stone when she shows her nocturnal face.

1 Data and Methods

1 INTRODUCTION

> Larvata prodeo: *I venture forth with a finger pointed to the mask: I put a mask on my feelings, but with a discreet (and deft) finger I point to the mask.*
>
> R. Barthes, *Fragments d'un discours amoureux*

There are human events that unfold in the dimly lit corners of the stage of life. What happens in those shadowy areas remains indistinct and subject to misinterpretation. Women and their affairs are relegated to those places, far from centre stage, far from the spotlight, which is always directed elsewhere, towards others. The life of women, even when filled with tragedy and violence, is played out in those places, where facile judgements, undue simplifications and recurrent misunderstandings reign in a world of stereotypes and indeterminacy. The meaning of violence for women is unclear and the meaning of actions that do not fall into established behavioural schemes eludes us. Those who attempt an explanation tend merely to reveal the misconceptions on which their arguments are founded. Some view women's entry into the underworld of violence, a world culturally alien to them, as proof of their attainment of equality with the other sex, as proof of the demolition of old barriers erected by the male world to defend its prerogatives; others condemn it in the name of preconceived notions that lack any tenable grounding.

Whatever the case, the fact is that participation in violent crime has never benefited the cause of women. When Voltaire declared, in 1743, that the time had come when a poet had the duty and women the power to be boldly *philosophe*, he was certainly not thinking of equality in terms of freedom to assume roles inspired by violence. But he did envisage the emergence of a new and different kind of woman on the cultural scene, one that finally would be illuminated in her positive diversity. Instead, very little would be conceded to women by the revolution of luminaries; the offensive of the *raison* in fact set out to free men of their chains, not women. Their 'diversity', intended as inferiority, was to remain a firmly anchored concept even during that extraordinary historical period. If attention turned to women it was

1

only to define their boundaries. Rousseau, who advanced his career by frequenting salons hosted by enlightened women, recalled women to their domestic duties and proscribed their access to knowledge. In the end, as Olympe de Gouges concluded, the only right the French Revolution gave women was the right to the guillotine.

The more recent experiences of women have also been negative. Women's participation in the union struggles in England, in the 1914–1918 War and in the Resistance during the Second World War once again proves that the only right readily accorded to them is the right to self-sacrifice and martyrdom. The historical lesson to be drawn from the methods of violent struggle adopted by feminist movements in England, beginning with the union struggles of the early 1800s and on with the suffragette movement, is that women end up fighting and sacrificing themselves for causes they later discover are not theirs. The unions accepted women, took their union dues, but ran their organisations without consulting them and, finally, excluded them from the work world at the end of the war (Rowbotham, 1974).

Yet, in spite of a culture that insists on relegating them to the limbo of a daily routine filled with small things and small deeds, women tragically persist in reappearing on the scene of violence and death. It is difficult to understand the profound meaning of this obstinate will. For some, the involvement of women in homicidal violence is a sign of rejection of their own identity, the surrender to that irrepressible drive that La Boétie called 'voluntary servitude', meaning lack of a true free-will. According to this view, yielding to these drives is a negation of feminine values and the culture of women which is, necessarily, the culture of life.

For others – the feminists in particular – this confusion over roles, tragically mixing the meaning of creating life with that of dispensing death, is undoubtedly problematic, but, everything considered, is accepted as inevitable.

It should strike us as strange that such important aspects of the life experience of the female half of the human species are shrouded in mystery, interpreted on the basis of suppositions, hypotheses and personal feelings. The truth is that much is said about women, but little is known about them. The lack of interest, especially at the scientific level, in certain unexpected responses of women to certain social problems is proof of this. For example, widely available statistics on drug dependency clearly indicate that women addicts do not exceed 15–18% of the drug-dependent population. Yet we still do not understand why women resist this extreme form of victimisation better than men, although the fact is certainly significant.

Similarly – and here we come to the heart of the matter we are concerned with – we have yet to understand why women who have participated in armed subversive movements have shown greater resistance than men to penitentism. Even in this case the data are unambiguous: it is simply a matter of understanding and interpreting them. But this diversity between men's and women's response to penitentism, which is surely critical to understanding the problem of terrorism in general as well how to control it, has been strangely ignored. To our knowledge, no one has noted this particular fact (and rivers of ink have flowed on the subject of terrorism) and, if noted, it was not deemed worthy of mention or study. This lack of attention is demonstrated by the fortuitous circumstances that led to our focusing on this peculiar fact. The starting point for this inquiry was not, as is usually the case, an outside stimulus (a statistical datum, a scientific article or a news item), but our simple impression that women defendants in trials for subversion were less disposed than men to 'collaborate' with the justice authorities. The general impression that there were fewer women among the ranks of the 'penitents' was confirmed by our study. Indeed, the data presented in the next section based on a study of a considerable amount of case material on the main terrorist movements in Italy prove that there are fewer women than men among the ranks of the 'penitents'. This finding, we must say, was somewhat surprising, since the cultural stereotypes that still inform the social perception of women (weak, dependent on the male universe, inconsistent, irrational, instinctive, suggestionable) would have led us to predict the contrary, that is, a greater disposition on women's part to repentance, collaboration and avoidance of incarceration. But having proven this unexpected diversity between the sexes, we shifted the focus of our inquiry from verification to interpretation of our hypothesis. And in order to give the data the 'weight' of a meaningful difference between the male and female perspective on involvement in such a serious and alarming form of criminality as political subversion, further study was called for. Indeed, the fact that there are fewer women than men among the ranks of the 'penitents' could have been attributed to a variety of factors, such as the insignificant number of women involved in armed subversion, the 'lower profile' of penitent women, due perhaps to the fact that the press focused on male penitentism or the relative unimportance of the information obtainable from female sources given the marginal positions women presumably held in the subversive organisations. Therefore, after confirming on the basis of judicial material that women actually were more resistant to penitentism, we set out to ascertain the positions actually held by women in subversive organisations and to analyse the meaning of their participation in armed struggle.

2   COMPILATION AND ANALYSIS OF CASE MATERIAL

The review of the case material (approximately 15,000 pages) required considerable effort to distinguish between persons categorised as 'penitent' (*pentiti*), dissociated (*dissociati*) and obdurate (*irriducibili*) under Italian law.

We included among the penitents all those who took advantage of incentive laws, specifically, laws 15/80 and 304/82, which provided, unlike prior laws in the matter, sentence reduction to time served in cases of collaboration that furnished an exceptional contribution to the disbandment of armed groups. The new laws also provided for commutation of prison terms for those who dissociated themselves from armed struggle and, at the same time, exhibited 'loyalty to the justice system', furnishing the inquiring authorities with the names of companions who were still at large and specific information on where arms were stashed and meetings held. A 1987 law then provided for reduced sentences even for those who limited themselves to admitting their crimes, even though they declined to give the names of comrades still at large and for those who 'dissociated' themselves publicly from armed struggle. In the latter cases, however, the law was far less generous in reducing prison terms than in the case of active collaboration.

Our inquiry was conducted on the following judicial proceedings.

(1) Proceedings no. 225–81 against Corrado Alunni and 55 others regarding the activity of Communist Combat Formations (*Formazioni Combattenti Comuniste* [FCC]); Red Guerrillas (*Guerriglia Rossa* [GR]) and 28th of March Brigade (*Brigata XXVIII Marzo*);

(2) Proceedings no. 43/82 against Abbate Giovanni and 32 others concerning the activity of Communist Combat Formations and Armed Proletarian Squads (*Squadre Armate Proletarie* [SAP]); Communist Attack Detachments (*Reparti Comunisti d'Attacco* [RCA]);

(3) Proceedings no. 921/80 against Achilli Antonio and 175 others concerning the subversive activity of Pre-PL and Prima Linea

(PL) (Front Line); Communist Revolutionary Committees (*Comitati Comunisti Rivoluzionari* [COCORI]);

(4) Proceedings no. 231/82 against Achilli Antonio and 78 others concerning the activity of COCORI and Metropoli (Oreste Scalzone, etc.) and Gruppo Del Giudice; Gruppo Rapinatori (Armed Robbery Group) (Merendino, Finocchiello, Carnevali, etc.);

(5) Proceedings against Abbate Marino and 182 others concerning the activity of the armed group Prima Linea from 1976–1980, brought by the Procura della Repubblica di Torino (Turin Public Prosecutor);

(6) Proceedings no. 231–82 against Alieri Federico and 70 others concerning the activity of the Communists Organized for the Liberation of the Proletariat (*Comunisti organizzati per la liberazione del proletariato* [COLP]);

(7) Proceedings of 1984, by the Procura della Repubblica di Milano (Milan Public Prosecutor) against Adamoli and 111 others concerning the activity of the armed group Red Brigades-Walter Alasia Column (*Brigate Rosse-Colonna Walter Alasia* [BR-CWA]);

(8) Judgement of the Court of Assises of Rome against the accused in the Aldo Moro trial (Arreni and 62 others), including Barbara Balzerani, Mario Moretti, Adriana Faranda, Valerio Morucci, Natalia Ligas and Antonio Savasta.

As we can see, the sample examined includes the Red Brigades in its two formations – the one that answered to the national command (Moretti and Balzerani) and the one that broke off from that command at the meeting of Tor San Lorenzo and acted independently thereafter (the Walter Alasia Column), the Prima Linea and the Communist Combat Formations.

Thus, these are groups, such as the Red Brigades, which defined themselves from the beginning as 'armed bands' and practiced terrorism through political assassination to eliminate obstacles posed by the State to the institution of the dictatorship of the proletariat and independent subversive groups that practiced 'the ideology of the executing counter-power' and did not immediately engage in a head-on clash with capitalism, in the belief it was more important at first to constitute an opposition power by increasing the 'clash level' of the union struggles under way.

Bruno Laronga, the historical leader of Prima Linea, clarifies the difference between the theoretical and practical conception of these two groups in this way:

> Our conception of avant-garde armed struggle consisted, at least in its intention, in a dialectical process between us – the central organization – and the movement; its intention was to develop the force starting from the bottom, based on the direct needs of the proletariat in the local districts; in essence the organization was envisaged as a service to, and for the self-defense of, the movement. The kidnapping and murder of the Honorable Moro, the fruit of *dirigisme* and the Leninist concept of the role of the armed organization, of the party that arrogates to itself the conscience and direction of the class, is the point of no return for all armed organizations, for the movements themselves and for the small scattered groups over which we sought to impose our direction. Our concept, which saw military operativity grow in the country, in the 'militia', stood in opposition to that of the 'apparatus' of the Red Brigades, of the State against the State, which was totally alien to us. (Di Carmelo, 1989)

The numerical data we obtained are reported in Table 1.1 and Figure 1.1. These show the relationship between male and female penitents: the women penitents (13 out of 100) numbered approximately half the number of men penitents (24 out of 100).

3   WOMEN'S PARTICIPATION IN ARMED SUBVERSION

In order to interpret the percentage data set out above, some clarification concerning the role women actually played within the subversive groups is in order.

Of those who at one time or another were among the leadership of Prima Linea (Turinese Command, Milanese Command and National Executive) three were women; Susanna Ronconi, Giulia Borelli and our interviewee Silveria Russo. None collaborated with the authorities other than to admit to the crimes of which they were accused and to dissociate themselves from armed struggle. Among the men there was the 'super penitent' Giai.

Of the armed bands, the COLP (Communists Organized for the Liberation of the Proletariat) had the highest percentage of women overall

Table 1.1

Groups	Total	Men	Women	Penitent men	Penitent women
FCC+XXVIII	56	45 (80%)	11 (20%)	17 (37%)	3 (27%)
FCC+SAP+RCA	35	25 (71%)	10 (29%)	5 (20%)	0 (0%)
PrePL+PL+RCA	175	151 (86%)	21 (14%)	35 (23%)	3 (12%)
PL	183	152 (83%)	31 (17%)	38 (25%)	6 (19%)
COLP+NC	79	48 (67%)	23 (33%)	11 (22%)	0 (0%)
COCORI+Metropoli	79	69 (87%)	10 (13%)	17 (25%)	2 (20%)
BR – CWA	112	77 (69%)	35 (31%)	23 (29%)	6 (17%)
BR-Processo Moro	63	46 (73%)	17 (27%)	4 (8%)	2 (11%)
Total	774	613 (79%)	161 (20%)	150 (24%)	22 (13%)

Notes: Chi square: 8.61 per *p* between 0.01 and 0.001. The chi square test confers further statistical significance to a difference that is already 'visibly' significant: 8.61 with a level of probability between *p* = 0.01 and *p* = 0.001 means that there is approximately one probability in 100 to err.

FFC = Formazioni Combattenti Comuniste (Communist Combat Formations)
XXVIII = Brigata XXVIII Marzo (28th March Brigade)
SAP = Squadre Armate Proletarie (Armed Proletarian Squads)
RCA = Reparti Comunisti d'Attacco (Communist Attack Detachments)
Pre-PL
  and PL = Prima Linea (Front Line)
COLP = Comunisti Organizzati per la Liberazione del Proletariato (Communists Organized for the Liberation of the Proletariat)
COCORI = Comitati Comunisti Rivoluzionari (Communist Revolutionary Committees)
GR = Guerriglia Rossa (Red Guerrillas)
BR = Brigate Rosse (Red Brigades)
BR–CWA = Brigate Rosse–Colonna Walter Alasia (Red Brigades–Walter Alasia Column).

(33%) and a prevalence of women in the command structure of the organisation. None of the women collaborated with the authorities, though many later dissociated themselves, such as Susanna Ronconi and Giulia Borelli (Guicciardi, 1988).

The Red Brigades-Walter Alasia Column had a much more hierarchical structure than Prima Linea, especially with the onset of the Balzerani–Moretti leadership. There were five distinct successive leaderships of this column and women were always represented in proportion to their overall number in the column. In the first leadership, up to 1979, there was only Carla Brioschi with four men; in the second, between 1979 and 1980, there were two women, Betti Pasqua Aurora and Barbara Balzerani, and two men, Adamoli and Moretti; in the third, until February 1982, there was only one woman, Betti P. Aurora and one man, De Maria; in the fourth, from February 1982 to September

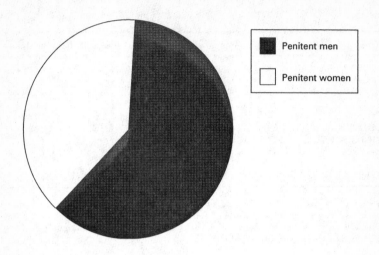

Figure 1.1

1982, there was one woman, Ettorina Zaccheo and three men, Carnelutti, Ferrari and Trombin; in the fifth, until the capture of nearly all the militants, there were two women, Ettorina Zaccheo and Daniela Rossetti and two men, Pasinelli and Bonato. There were no penitents among all those women; there were two penitents among the men.

Thus, the Red Brigades's leadership was composed over time by a total of 12 men and seven women; 16% of the men became penitents, while none of the women did.

But let us look at some organisational data. Participating in the leadership meant having responsibility for setting the political and operative agenda, deciding whom and where to strike, forming the organisation, deciding its rules and participating in the 'firing nuclei' (*nuclei di fuoco*) (Prima Linea) or in the 'operative nuclei' (*nuclei operativi*) (Red Brigades) and deciding who should be in and who should be 'kept on ice awaiting better times'. Even the terrorist movements geographically closest to Italy, in Germany, featured women in decision-making roles. It was their responsibility to decide whom to kidnap and whom to assassinate, to claim responsibility for terrorist actions, where to plant bombs, and to train like men in the Palestinian camps of Al Fatah. Although the men of the first generation of terrorists outnumbered the women (51 men to 39 women), the ideologues of the group were one man, Horst Mahler and one woman, Ulrike Meinhof and the levers of power were manned by women. The second generation of terrorists was prevalently composed of women (10 women to 6 men) who set for themselves the objective, before the armed-struggle phase (with the Committee Against the Torture of Political Prisoners) and during the active terrorist phase, of liberating 'political prisoners'. These ten women included Sigrid Sternebeck (who opted for transfer to West Germany in 1991 from East Germany, where she had been protected by STASI for 10 years) and her two friends Silke Maier-Witt and Susanne Albrecht.

No direct comparison is possible between Italian female penitentism and the German variety because the Bundestag only approved the *Kronzeugeregelung* for terrorist acts in 1989. German law provided for the reduction of sentences and even commutation to time served for former terrorists who actually collaborated with the justice authorities, but did not provide for the reduction of prison terms for those who merely dissociated themselves. Peter-Juergen Boock, who is serving a life sentence in the Hamburg prison, dissociated himself from armed struggle, but he can only hope that the President of the Federal Republic of Germany will grant his petition for clemency.

Thus, German penitentism only regards the second generation of terrorists. As of this writing we know that two men (Werner Lotze and Henning Beer) and two women (Susanne Albrecht and Silke Maier-Witt) have collaborated with the authorities (*Der Spiegel*, 13 August 1990). Since the women of the second generation of RAF terrorists outnumbered the men, the acts tend to prove that even in German terrorism fewer women than men opted for penitentism.

4 'PENITENTISM' AND ITS MEANING

> *Remorse is impotence; it will sin again. Only repentance is strong; it can end everything.*
>
> Henry Miller, 'Seraphita', *The Wisdom of the Heart*

A distinction should be made at the outset between 'penitentism' and repentance. Although both terms derive from the same Latin root, *paenitentia*, connoting sorrow and regret for wrongdoing, in Italian common usage the term 'penitent' (*pentito*) in the context of terrorism refers to a terrorist who dissociates himself or herself from armed struggle and collaborates with the justice authorities. Given this specific meaning of the term, motives are of secondary importance, although it is safe to say that the utilitarian component of penitentism probably outweighs the moral one of repentance. The currency of penitentism is bargaining and exchange. Repentance, on the other hand, is a gratuitous sentiment. If it produces any benefit, it is solely for the benefit of the repentant. It is difficult to say how much true repentance there is in an act of penitentism; and it is understandable that human justice should seek to avoid subtle distinctions based on personal motivation. In fact, despite common usage, judicial proceedings do not refer to penitents, but to defendants who exhibit 'procedural loyalty', that is, cooperation with the justice authorities (de Cataldo Neuburger, 1988). The only distinction at work in the law is a pragmatic one, distinguishing between credible and non-credible penitents, the latter notably comprising those involved in organised crime. Perhaps at the root of this distinction lies the notion that the terrorist does not pursue personal interests, but is moved by Utopian principles. The terrorist is assumed to operate in a sphere of moral coherence, however misguided and this makes him or her a credible penitent and, therefore, a credible witness. As Umberto Eco observed (*Espresso*, 5 October 1986), it is a respectable notion, defensible in many instances, but of dubious validity, as it was embraced by the justice system before it was thoroughly examined in the political and philosophical arena. Eco also expressed concern that the penitentism scheme precluded a finding of mental instability, immaturity or lability as explanations for terrorist activity, which, if true, would make penitent terrorists the least credible of all witnesses.

The 'respectable notion' of which Eco speaks has found its way into the thinking of some judges. Guicciardi, President of the Court of Appeal of Milan, states in *Il tempo del furore* (1988) that if there is a case in which we can recognise a true penitent, it is in the case of the terrorist who cherished an idea, the Utopia of a new world, or perhaps just of a new power, but not an idea tied to profit, revenge or drive. This person, according to Guicciardi, has few resources. Once his Utopia collapses, he may well choose to speed the end for himself and for others. He suffers a physical and moral collapse, which includes disappointment and a sudden understanding of the disproportion between the crime and the social benefit that may have been achieved.

If to this concept of terrorist as 'manqué moralist' we associate the 'moral value' of collaboration, we obtain the curious notion of the terrorist as negative hero, freed of his negative (criminal) charge and filled with positivity thanks to the intervention of the State. As Guicciardi goes on to state, we might say that this terrorist area, in which we grapple with social problems and deal with violence, led some to fanaticise these problems and attempt to resolve them with tragic simplification, but we certainly cannot deny the problems existed.

These thoughts, rich in human feelings and a sincere desire to understand, leave, however, unresolved the fundamental problem of distinguishing, albeit in the restricted context of criminal proceedings, between informer, penitent and socially redeemed. The reference criterion, rough and worn, is still based on the attribution of value to the motivation for the act. The equation is simple: if one is deemed to speak out of personal interest, he is an informer and, hence, dishonorable. The difference lies in the degree of baseness imputed to the act; one who collaborates out of noble motivations (expiation, reparation, confession) is a 'penitent', that is, one who has undergone profound interior change, one who has acknowledged to have sinned and seeks redemption. And the justice system duly acknowledges this process of intimate sufferance and desire for expiation and rewards the critical revision 'collaborants' visit on their past militancy. Penitents recognise they have sinned, they understand their errors, they confess them, and they desire to make reparation for the wrongs they have perpetrated. Among the former terrorists we interviewed, some chose the path of faith in addition to that of dissociation. For example, Silveria Russo, Mario Ferrandi and Bruno Laronga live repentance gratuitously. They do not flaunt it with public declarations. They bear witness to it through a life committed to service to others (Mario Ferrandi works, while under house arrest, to rehabilitate drug addicts and Silveria Russo and her husband Bruno Laronga work while on parole in a social services cooperative).

5 SURVEY METHODS

In order to investigate the specificity of female obduracy (*irriducibilità*), we prepared standardised multiple-choice questionnaires that were submitted to former terrorist women who agreed to be interviewed. After the first individual interview there was a second follow-up interview with both parties of terrorist couples. Among the former terrorists interviewed there were, in fact, two couples: Mara Aldrovandi (Communist Attack Detachments – *Reparti Comunisti d'Attacco*) and Mario Ferrandi (Prima Linea), and Silveria Russo and Bruno Laronga (Prima

Linea). The men were interviewed as well for two reasons: first, to test the hypothesis of women's greater resistance to repentance through their experience of women's participation in armed struggle; and, second, thanks to their willingness to dedicate time and effort to the task, to recollect the dialogue that took place between men and women in these terrorist groups.

The questionnaire was complemented by an unstructured interview in which the question of the interviewer depended on the preceding answer of the interviewee. The purpose that informed these questions and answers was not to reconstruct a life story or the motives for participating in armed struggle and for disassociating from it (as was the case in the questionnaire), but to explore the doubts and bring to light the contradictions that exist in the granite-like certitude that still encases the memory of armed militancy. In dealing with questions involving meaning, often implicit ('violence is a part of human nature' – Mara Aldrovandi) an attempt was made to place the meaning in a broader context of meanings that would allow for an alternative to the solution that was deemed inevitable. Thus, we answered Mara Aldrovandi's pronouncement with the following: 'But a mature and courageous human being engages in a struggle that keeps the adversary alive, in order that he or she may be recognised, even by the vanquished, as the victor. However risky this may have been, your experience as a union leader showed you that it is possible to obtain something even by "deferred conflict"...' (Appendix 2).

This free-form interview, which to some extent resembles a psychotherapy session, allowed us to evaluate the extent to which the subject had 'adjusted' to doubts about the role played (combatant or assassin?) and how some succeeded in living with an image of themselves as assassins while others tended to blunt the import of the crime by placing it in the context of the general violence of the situation.

This way of conducting the interviews also allowed us to play down the difference in roles, active for the interviewer and passive for the interviewee. Often the interviewer had to follow the lead of the interviewee. The reports on the interviews designate them as 'meetings' precisely because the interviews were structured from the beginning as meetings between two different viewpoints.

One last clarification. The results we obtained with our inquiry method (questionnaire and interview) are not proof of the effects of causes considered as independent variables. In fact, unlike a scientific experiment, our method of inquiry avoided quantitative manipulation of variable stimuli. It follows that the objectives of our inquiry were not demonstrative, but merely descriptive of 'states of affairs' or 'situations' that were already well-structured prior to our intervention (Canestrari, 1984).

We sought to compensate for diminished control in our inquiry method by gathering as much information as possible on the life stories of former terrorists from the memoirs of Russian terrorist women, from former terrorists of Prima Linea who participated in the Vallette Seminar held by Novelli and Tranfaglia (1988), from those who attended the seminar held by Bianca Guidetti Serra and Luisa Passerini (1988) and from the women terrorists who participated in meetings organised by the criminologist Malagutti (1987, 1988).

With regard to the preparation of the questionnaires, the first interview, that of 'F', served as a guideline and as a pre-test in preparing the actual questionnaire.

The conceptual framework on which we decided to focus attention is based on the relationship between 'gender identity', 'identification' and 'idealisation' and, therefore, on a theory of models broadened to psychoanalytic considerations on the typical psychological path of a terrorist. With respect to these three concepts the key questions were those that elicited (a) the portrayal of one's own cognitive and affective investment in the revolutionary cause, (b) the portrayal of oneself as an agent or instrument of the cause itself, (c) the portrayal of social groups for which one claims to have fought, and (d) the portrayal of the new society one sought to found.

With respect to (a) we found that the question in the pre-test submitted to F on the principal motive for her participation in armed struggle should have been more articulated to allow for alternative answers that would emphasise the sacrificial aspect (enamorment of the grand cause) rather than awareness of the historical trend under way (profound conviction in the rightness of the cause) and the maniacal dimension of the commitment (sense of one's own greatness).

With respect to (b) we decided to eliminate the term 'portrayal' to elicit the immediate life experience and not an elaboration of it. Interviewee F thought the term was too removed from her actual participation in Prima Linea. Moreover, reading the life stories in the report on the Vallette Seminars (1988), such as that of Ronconi, we thought terms such as 'portrayal' could lend themselves to casual manipulation on the part of subjects who were particularly inclined to ideologising everything that is 'knowable and doable'. The portrayal of social groups on behalf of which one claimed to fight and of the new society one wanted to create (c and d) is reflected in all the questions and serves to identify the affective code by which the subject lived armed subversion.

As we mentioned, the questionnaire for couples was prepared with a second meeting in mind which would have the dual objective of gathering, on the one hand, as many facts as possible on what inspired militant men as opposed to militant women and, on the other, of encouraging dialogue between the two subjects to elicit what was still alive of the old motivations, how their life projects had changed, etc.

The research and the interviews were submitted in their preliminary form to the subjects interviewed. Only F refused further meetings. Further interviews and meetings followed to correct inaccuracies and omissions and to delve more deeply into areas of particular concern to the interviewees.

For ease of consultation the questionnaires and interviews are reported in the appendices at the end of this book.

6 PSYCHOLOGICAL CRITERIA OF INTERPRETATION

We employed a number of interpretative instruments to analyse the material gathered through the questionnaires and interpret it according to the various psychological levels of interpretation suggested by the material itself. In particular, in order to identify the relationships between gender identity, identification and idealisation, our psychological inquiry started at the tip of the iceberg. We started, that is, from the more general and 'visible' aspects of these phenomena and proceeded to the well-defended psychic areas below the waterline. The use of varied interpretative models was dictated by the course we undertook to pursue. Having abandoned the main thoroughfare of interpretation, we had to make our way down a difficult path fraught with perilous concepts of uncertain psychological interpretation. Thus, for the inquiry on gender identity, which is the first level of analysis, we employed interpretative instruments of general psychology and of the study of female specificity. The inquiry on the destiny of the identifications of the young women who become adults called for the use of interpretative instruments from development psychology. Recourse to this particular perspective was justified by the fact that the average age of the defendants in terrorist trials ranged from 22 to 28 years; in some instances the defendants joined terrorist groups before reaching adulthood. People like Adamoli and Fenzi were exceptions to the rule. As public prosecutor Armando Spataro stated at the Tobagi trial, political militancy in extreme left-wing groups, especially in Workers' Power (*Potere Operaio*) (which according to the public prosecutor of the Public Prosecutor's Office of Milan was the strain from which the leaders of the Red Brigades and Workers' Independence [*Autonomia Operaia*] evolved), preceded armed militancy and set the stage for it. Militants in terrorist organisations north of the Alps were also young. The first generation of RAF terrorists was composed of young people who severed ties with their families and went underground at approximately 22–23 years of age. The average age shifts to 28–30 years for second-generation terrorists (June 2nd Movement), who were, however, at least to some extent those who constituted the friendship network for the historical nucleus of the Bader-Meinhof Band (*Der Spiegel*, 11 May 1981).

Finally, the most complex and problematic aspect, that of idealisation, calls into play the psychology of defence mechanisms, that is, all the pre-conscious strategies that the ego adopts in order to survive and not suffer the devastating effects of its own drives. As we know, these consist of mechanisms that operate at nearly inaccessible depths that can only be analysed with the help of psychological models capable of overcoming the threshold at which other interpretative criteria exhaust their explicative efficacy. On the other hand, feminine psychology (and here we return to the question of gender identity) predisposes women to certain defence mechanisms rather than to others. If a woman can withstand the hatred of a son better than his unsatisfied hunger for love, it is because introversion of aggressivity is a prevalently feminine defence mechanism (Deutsch, 1977).

Thus, depth psychology offers perhaps the most exhaustive model in the field of psychology, since it lends itself to different ways of describing and explaining human conduct (in this case the behaviour and life experiences of militant terrorists) into a broader conceptual framework. In practice, the psychoanalytic model was employed as the conceptual framework of an inquiry conducted with the help of a number of models, each of which made a specific contribution to understanding various aspects of the matter. The cognitive model, for example, that is, the heterogeneous complex of research on knowledge and its levels (perception, discrimination, categorisation and problem-solving) has, on the one hand, given experimental confirmation of the defence mechanisms which are thought to be at work in armed militants and, on the other hand, it demonstrated, by negative inference, that the cognitive investment in terrorist actions is insignificant compared to the overpowering affective investment. The history of terrorism confirms this. Workers appreciated the political struggles fought on their behalf against businesses by union leader Mara Aldrovandi, but they gained no benefit from her armed militancy-and, hence, did not offer her any 'reinforcement'. The murders, kneecappings and kidnappings of heads of personnel failed to stop factory lay-offs in the North; this is the reason why the labour movement never gave any 'social reinforcement' to De Maria of the Walter Alasia Column for violent action, while it did support the initiatives, even some harsh ones, of factory councils. The lack of support on the part of the great majority of the labour movement for those who wanted to institute a proletariat dictatorship (Red Brigades) or a new free and democratic society, especially for workers, should have been warning enough of the utter impracticability of armed struggle. If the militant groups went ahead notwithstanding, as they did, for example, by killing Dr Marangoni because he constituted an obstacle to the proletariat's control of the health care system, it was because the support of those outside their own group, the workers included, was of little interest to the Red Brigades and the members of Organized Independence (*Autonomia Organizzata*).

At this point our inquiry reaches its most difficult phase, that of examining the complex material obtained from the questionnaires and interviews in search of an explanation for women's participation in armed subversion. To make progress in this area we made use of yet another psychological tool, the 'affective code'. If by code we mean a system to preserve and transmit information from stored data in a range of possible arrangements (Fornari, 1976), we may define the affective code as an arrangement of affective information and a system of affective evaluations, that is, a range of possible choices which, in the final analysis, are a range of decisional options. They might be said to 'give shape', from the inside, to an individual's perception of himself and of the world, thereby generating knowledge and action.

According to this theory, such codes predispose to affective behaviour that is, in essence, sexual or parental (Maggiolini, 1988).

The 'filial code' is characterised by unconscious drives of appropriation and omnipotence; the fundamental features of the 'maternal code' are devotion, kindness and 'sacrificing competency'; the 'paternal code' emphasises duties, authority and reality; and the 'fraternal code' governs the symmetrical and parity relations within a group context.

The interviews in Chapter 4 contain many examples of the functioning of maternal (M) and paternal (P) affective codes:

(M) 'My comrades had only an instrumental relationship with me: **I was useful to them and I was glad that I was useful to them, that I was indispensable to them. That was really it, the fact that I was indispensable to them.**' ('F')

(P) 'As compared with that experience', says Mario Ferrandi, 'I now miss not being able to unmask the hypocrisy of the powerful as we were doing then, and the subservience of the press. **Then I had some effect, but not any more.**'

(P) '**To have an impact on the life of society. To exercise real power. The pleasure of exercising a real counterpower:** we blew up the rails of the Metro because we wanted to participate in the festivities of the Ascension.' (Ferrandi)

(M) 'For me, it is the collective aspect that I miss most, **the fact that I was not alone, that I was accepted and could talk about everything.** This was true, however, only of my militancy before the armed struggle, because in the armed struggle I could only talk about fliers and goals.' (Mara Aldrovandi)

(M) '... when you have faith you can keep going even without concrete results...' (Mara Aldrovandi)

(M) '**Yes, I knew that... they were using me, but I was glad to be used because I was working for a worthwhile cause..**'

(M) '**They needed me and I let myself be used. I was satisfied with that.**' (Mara Aldrovandi)

(P) (M) 'My father was the only male figure. He was a typical head of family **who knew how to resolve difficult situations,** and whenever he had time he stayed with us and gave us time and attention. My father let me travel a good deal. My mother was the **classical attentive mother who managed the family with tenderness and strength.**' (Mara Aldrovandi)

(M) 'The women **sublimated crises with efforts at solidarity.** In every crisis they knew how to bring the men and women together.' (Mara Aldrovandi)

(P) 'I repented,' says Mara, 'if we want to use that term, **because**

in the name of what was I supposed to do 15 years in prison, **now that there was no longer any motivation** whatever for armed struggle, much less for prison. Instead I got myself arrested. . . .'

Other statements emphasise the characteristics of women's involvement in armed struggle.

'We wanted to create a more just society, but we ourselves did not become more just, we did not mature, we did not progress, and the yardstick of progress is oneself: we never talked about intimate things, personal things and that would have been a good thing to do. **The women lost their true character, they were just women combatants; it was the men who mostly ran things** and affections had to be kept at bay because one of the partners might unexpectedly wind up in hiding. Stability in affections was a privilege few had.' ('F')

'We were convinced that we could not do differently, that we had to use violence; there was no room for anything else. I said this to the feminists of Turin too, who had made a non-violent choice **that would have been a normal choice for a woman.**' (Silveria Russo)

'. . . there was no female commander and **in any case aptitude for command is masculine** . . .' (Bruno Laronga)

'**Women lacked ready initiative, the strength to lead** . . .'

'I can tell you that women would not have put Moro on trial. There is a kind of political cynicism **that only men have**. In Potere Operaio (Workers Power) **we were not anti-feminist, but we took into consideration attitudes toward combat and command** when it was a question of choosing a woman to work with. Sex did not enter into it at all at that point. **Women are moralists, with a visceral kind of moralism that history, at least, is not made with:** in practice, women take part in the armed struggle because of all the violence they have suffered.' (Mario Ferrandi)

'In the armed struggle women had to win equality because and, let us not forget it, **violence has always been masculine and women have always been subjected to it.**' (Mario Ferrandi)

'To judge feminine repentance you have to begin with one's joining the armed struggle, **which for women is something to weigh up much more than for men, because women have more at stake**

than men [. . .] I am sure that for a woman to give up motherhood is terrible, the idea of not marrying because there is no time for it is terrible. A man does not have motherhood at stake. **In a word, women think it over three times as much before joining the armed struggle.**' (Mara Aldrovandi)

'There can be a personality structure that predisposes one to less resistance to stressful events like vaginal examinations in prison, the fact that you were allowed only 1 hour out in the fresh air, that the surveillance on you was of a particularly persecutory character. Faced with these circumstances, **I never gave any indication of yielding**, nor did persons who might perhaps seem vulnerable, like CZ.' (Silveria Russo)

'A person who puts the safety of others at risk is a bad person, but I can understand a woman comrade of the Red Brigades involved in the Dozier kidnapping, who, after having been kept in prison for 15 days with a bullet in her leg, said: "Forgive me, comrades, but I cannot stand it any longer!" I never heard a man say anything like that.' (Mara Aldrovandi)

The feminist movement has concentrated on one affective code in particular, the maternal–sacrificial code, in its search for the roots of female oppression. The maternal code, that is, the response to needs founded on the principle of giving all and taking nothing, which is genetically determined because useful to the survival of the child (Maggiolini, 1988), has always enjoyed considerable social support according to Fedeli (1982), because the sacrificial attitude of the mother allows the man to manage the socio-economic and political–legal power without worrying about the management of the family microsystem and to develop initiative, power, daring and competitivity without dispersing energy in assisting the bedridden elderly, defenceless children and the dying – in other words, without developing empathy for the limitedness of the human condition. Thus, the maternal code explains in an emotive–affective key a system of relationships that is more complex than is evidenced by the sociopolitical interpretation of sexual roles. The women's movement acquired one very important insight from this, that is, that the male sociocultural system assailed by feminists in reality rests on a maternal type of symbolic order, which goes a long way in explaining the solidity of the patriarchy (Fedeli, 1982).

A number of explanatory models, therefore, are subsumed under the psychodynamic model and used according to their specific explicative possibilities. This arrangement, which some may view as unprincipled, but which served as a stepping-stone to address the fundamental question of this inquiry, that is, the reasons for women's greater resistance, is possibly due to the two currents of thought that have informed psychology since its appearance on the scientific scene in the nineteenth century. They were the Galilean current, that is, the need for science to better control the forces of nature and the Baconian current, that is, 'the need to know oneself and perceive oneself better' (Soro, 1991).

These two currents have justified multifaceted observational practices and, therefore, conceptual frameworks.

Experimental psychology (the Galilean current) was pioneered by Wundt, founder of the first laboratory of experimental psychology in Europe in 1879 (the Leipzig Laboratory). It uses the methodology of the natural sciences, that is, it makes use of the observational instruments of physiology and the procedure of reducing psychological experience to its simplest and most elementary elements (sensation, perception, discrimination reaction, and so on). This methodological framework, however, does not preclude distinguishing between the object of the natural sciences and the object of the psychological disciplines: the former, abstracted from any link with the subject, makes recourse to an auxiliary concept such as matter, while the latter, considered immediate experience, is the result of mingling objective and subjective data. The complex nature of the psychological phenomenon has a definite bearing on the procedures available to investigate the 'properly subjective'. Since the objectification of observational technologies is the only procedure that allows for intersubjective verification or refutation, psychology today is characterised by stronger and weaker models, depending on the degree of their verifiability. For example, cognitivism and behaviourism, which make extensive use of experimental psychology, are considered strong models, while psychoanalysis, clinical psychology and psychopathology are viewed as weak models. The object of the strong models is designated by the observational practices themselves, therefore it lends itself to infinite reproduction; the object of the weak models is not concretised, but unfolds over time as a search for meaning and integration of the 'black holes' of the ego.

There is disagreement between the supporters of the clinical method and the experimental method even regarding the issue of quantification, which pervades the entire experimental approach. It is not just a question of elaborating and generalising the results so as to infer 'regionally' valid laws expressed in mathematical language amenable to statistical analysis, but of designing the research – in the formulation of hypotheses, the manipulation of independent variables and the use of levels of experience – in a quantified and quantifiable manner. According to the clinical method, it is only possible to quantify what can be placed along a continuous dimension. Man and, above all, the unconscious aspects of his behaviour, are not amenable to that: every aspect of the individual psyche has an irreducible nucleus that experimental quantification risks to distort (Cesa-Bianchi, 1987).

As we can see, the history of psychology 'sees in the facts an instance of shattering the empirical subject into the multifacetedness of the practices that the various theories counterpose from the outset' (Soro, 1991).

Those who seek the reasons – and not just superficial ones – underlying human conduct and seek to understand, as we do in this inquiry, the reason for a phenomenon which resonated loudly on the social scene but has its true roots in the depths of the psyche, must retrace the path step by step, from the macrosystem to the exosystem and on to depth psychology to avoid incorrect reductions.

2 The Phenomenon, the Context and the People

1 THE MEANING OF VIOLENCE

Without violence you obtain nothing; violence has to be answered with violence, there is no other way.

Mara Aldrovandi (Appendix 2)

Violence is scandalous, but it rests on the same theoretical foundation and structure of the social world itself. It is an important component of our collective memory; indeed, many archetypes are cultivated on a substratum of violence. Moral conscience is grounded in the great original taboos, incest and the killing of the totemic animal, which concludes the tragic course of the cyclopic family intuited by Freud. The cultural premises of our society are deeply rooted in the primordial magma that flows deep in the unconscious. It surfaces in Greek mythology, in which men retrieve and externalise ancient fantasies constructed around violence and cruelty in order to exorcise them. The powers that be in the heavens and on earth as they were 'conceived' by men seem moved only by perverse instincts: patricide, fratricide, cannibalism and incest. From the blood of Uranus, emasculated by his son Chronos, were born the Erinyes. The gods seem indifferent to injustice and oppression. This explains why we will always find, in the past and for centuries to come, an act of genuine illegitimacy, a violent drama, at the root of any formal legitimacy. Romulus killed Remus and founded Rome. There is no reign, city, dynasty or ideological movement that does not have its skeletons in the closet. Even Christianity begins with a crucifixion that has all the air of a judicial error. In other words, violence is not a metaphysical category. It is an ancient message, engraved in our genetic code since time immemorial, ever current and stimulating. Violence is fascinating. It is an inexhaustible reserve of energy. It excites us, it makes us feel alive, it breaks the monotony of daily routine, it dispels loneliness, it cures feelings of impotence and helplessness.

Violence is cathartic. Some maintain that it is educational. In the past, torture and capital punishment took place in public to serve as an example and an admonishment. Violence has a thousand faces: violence against the elderly and women, violence by young people, violence in situations and emotions, violence in images that 'banalise' violence itself and make it appear 'normal' behaviour, instrumental violence, premeditated, gratuitous, ludic, demonstrative, more or less 'visible', individual, collective and group violence, and violence by the State (de Cataldo Neuburger, 1987).

The instrument is too subtle and refined, too exquisitely calibrated and tuned to be a banal accident along the evolutionary path of the human species.

2 SUBVERSIVE VIOLENCE AND ITS SOCIODEMOGRAPHIC CONTEXT

> *What will we do when we meet Martians? The answer that first comes to mind, especially if by 'mind' we mean the subconscious, is* Shoot.
>
> V. Mathieu

In truth, the theory of a more or less banal accident along the way has been embraced by many thinkers to exorcise frightening visions of armed subversion. These people believe it is absurd to have violent protest, meaning aphasic–analogical communication in the political sphere, in countries in which technological development is exalted and numerical–verbal communication has triumphed. They admit such violence may have some effect, but they view it as imprecise and anti-economical and dramatic evidence of man's mistrust in his best resources (Calvi, 1982).

A survey by Calvi and Martini (1982) on the attitude of Italians toward violence, with reference in particular to its ideological and pragmatic components and its relative value, shows, on the basis of a representative sample of 5,000 Italians aged 15–64 years, that at least 4,000,000 Italians approve the instrumental value of political violence, 9,000,000 would refuse to collaborate with the police in the fight against terrorism, and 750,000 are tired of waiting, and would abandon all moderation and would refuse to collaborate with the justice authorities.

This benign attitude towards violence cannot be viewed as an *ad hoc* position taken for the survey, as it correlates with significant sociodemographic traits and specific structures of social values.

With regard to sociodemographic traits, the positive attitude towards political violence – already well entrenched in persons under 17 years of age (14.5%) – actually increases in the population up to the age of 24 years (14.9%) and decreases thereafter (6% at 64 years of age). Moreover, the percentage increases with the level of education: 8.3% among those with an elementary school diploma versus 12.8% among those with a university degree.

It also varies as a function of left–right political orientation: 5.5% for the right, 6.1% for the centre, 10.3% for the centre–left and 22.7% for the left.

Value orientation, on the other hand, met with a very low consensus (5.9%) compared to expectations (30%). The first entry in the survey ('Collaboration between social classes is a pious illusion; it is through violence that any progress is made') directly refers to the notion of class struggle and ought in theory to be set out as a fundamental social value for those who side with the left.

The statistical data offer immediate verification of the sociohistorical principle enunciated by Bossle (1978), according to which recourse to radical violence is and has been throughout the history of revolutions in Europe, a privilege of the bourgeoisie and of the aristocracy and not of the proletariat. If the principle of ideological legitimisation of violence exercised by an oppressed class to overcome the hegemony of a dominant class meets with only modest consensus, the explanation probably lies in the decay of the ideological, class-oriented inspiration for violence, on the one hand, and in the affirmation of a pragmatic, anarchic–individualistic creed, on the other, according to which one is free to defend oneself as best one can and may resort to any means to protect one's rights.

Calvi (1982) maintains that the idealistic notions underlying terrorism that seem to have touched the hearts of 4,000,000 Italians must be based on the belief that groups of people have a right to fight all others in society without regard for any civil or moral rules. Perhaps Calvi's (1982) conclusions require further explanation, because formulated in this way they fail to explain the behaviour of individual terrorists who were actually strongly motivated by ideology, so much so that they attributed the tragic quality of their actions to it. We say tragic, not criminal, because for them the objective was idealistic. Specifically, they sought the liberation of the oppressed classes from exploitation and abuse; but the means chosen, political assassination and knee-capping, in the end corrupted both the objective and the people themselves. To give an example, the ideological, class-oriented inspiration for the killing of Marangoni, Medical Director of the Milan Policlinic, was, according to the flyer claiming authorship of the action published by the Walter Alasia Column of the Red Brigades, to reclaim control of the health care system by the proletariat, as it was being usurped by the bourgeoisie in the form of plans to restructure the management of the system. Similarly, the ideological inspiration for the wounding of the female prison guard RN, according to Silveria Russo (Appendix 7), was deterrence against mistreatment of women prisoners by the bourgeois power and punishment of this particular woman prison guard for excessive zeal on the job. The ideological inspiration remained an idea only. It was never realised in concrete steps to keep bourgeois management out of the health care system, nor was an alternative management system proposed and while inhuman incarceration was condemned, no alternative prison structure was proposed. Without a programme to enact an idea, to give it flesh and bones, it remains in the realm of fetishistic absoluteness and, as such, it dictates and justifies the destruction of any obstacle that casts a shadow on its metaphysical splendor. Lack of a programme means lack of negation, as Funke (1978) noted. It is thus conceivable that to compensate for the lack of negation one could be led to the greatest negation of all, that of life.

Bruno Laronga's 'lack of ideological and class-oriented inspiration in favour of a sort of armed individualism' (Appendix 7) is now perhaps clearer and can be explained as an 'aristocratic attitude' (Bruno Laronga, Appendix 9) or a 'heroic' attitude (Mario Ferrandi, Appendix 10) or as the deliverance from oppression by the State and the 'enterprise command' (Bruno Laronga, Appendix 7).

This is how Silveria Russo explains it:

I think that a hypothesis was made rather than hatching a well-formed sociopolitical design; the design actually was the Utopia of a better society (Communist? Yes, but I think without even knowing what it meant... Therefore we can say that many of us were generally in favour of a 'more just world' without exploitation... I would therefore say that the compression of reason and anti-reason was there right from the beginning, in the desire to realise a Utopia (specific and community oriented) while believing that only violence is the 'leavening of history' (and this is a specific ideological reference)... without the separation that exists between the design (lucid and Apollonian) and the reality of men who must effect it; there was the reality of men because the design was there in the first place. (See Appendix 13)

Vincenza Fioroni (Appendix 11) echoes her affirmation that, indeed, armed struggle meant for her the creation of a more just society, even though, she says:

I wasn't clear about the kind of future society. There wasn't a model to emulate even amongst socialist societies; the desire for justice and freedom was more far-ranging and radical than could be contained and realised in a totalitarian state.

A survey similar to Calvi's was carried out in the Federal Republic of Germany by an infratest on commission by the Ministry of Internal Affairs on a representative sample of 4,000 individuals ranging from 16 to 50 years of age.

The results, presented by Calvi and Martini (1982), show that 4.4% of the sample was capable of left-wing protest. This group mainly comprised young people with a high level of education, still insecure and poorly integrated in society from an economic standpoint. Economic insecurity alone, however, cannot explain the propensity for political protest, since fulfillment of material needs on the whole was considered less important for this group than the average for the entire population. In fact, this group was oriented towards post-materialistic values (such as, according to the survey, self-realisation through work that allows for the full development of one's skills and creativity). According to Calvi (1982), the survey shows that the perception of economic insecurity reinforces criticism of the political system and that the 'deprivation of ideals', that is, an ever clearer awareness of the gap between reality and values learned in the educational process, can lead to political radicalisation, especially in the case of highly educated individuals.

This comment on the statistical data is supported by several articles on men and women terrorists of the *Rote Armee Fraction* in the German weekly *Der Spiegel*. Virtually all the terrorists were from upper-middle-class families (lawyers, businessmen, career military personnel) and, in some instances, from 'enlightened' families concerned with the needs of the 'unprotected' and disenfranchised. The very wealthy Grete Albrecht, grandmother of Susanne Albrecht, the actual executrix of the assassination of the banker Ponto, was a 'doctor of the poor', a Social Democrat by tradition; Gudrun Ennslin grew up in a religious family and was very sensitive to the suffering of those who did not participate in the well-being of West Germany's affluent society; Ulrike

Meinhof, one of the high-profile members of the Bader-Meinhof band was brought up by a brilliant left-wing professor, Renate Reimeck.

The men and women terrorists of the RAF were people with university degrees or studying for their degrees, and most of them, before going underground, were engaged in professions that put them in contact with marginalised people, the 'unprotected' and the suffering. Juliane Plambeck was a nurse in the Red Rescue Squad (*Soccorso Rosso*), and Elizabeth von Dyck looked after the legal interests of patients as a class, founding a collective for the defence of psychiatric patients from institutionalisation for mental disorders in Heidelberg in 1970. All of them worked at these different professions with a high degree of motivation that was not attributable solely to the economic advantage they gained from them – when they weren't actually working for free (*Der Spiegel*, 8 August 1977, 13 August 1990).

This culture of total dedication and commitment to the victims of capitalist exploitation (Bruno Laronga: see Appendix 9), of the desire to integrate disenfranchised social minorities, of the more or less Utopian aspirations for a better world, slowly became a culture of the most brutal violence. Of course, the social ferment under way in that period tended, for better or for worse, to support these social dynamics. In 1968, *Les Lettres Francaises* published a special issue devoted to student movements; this is the statement of a woman, a philosophy student:

I find it exciting that so many people, myself included, rebelled, simply rebelled. It was somewhat successful because we did not have a well-defined ideology at the outset, only a general attitude of opposition – against the police, against order, against society. It was something asocial . . . it really was the desire for novelty, or change: it was this desire that began to take shape as violence . . . everyone understands it, everyone feels it.

When this undefined difficulty in accepting the values of culture and, therefore, integration into society, which in the initial phase gave way to manifestations of generalised malaise and a desire for opposition, became awareness and commitment to awaken the conscience of other social groups, there was a need for a deeper conceptual framework for protest which soon became a need for a head-on collision with the institutional powers to be destroyed.

3 THE FACES OF TERRORISM

What is terrorism to some is heroism to others.

Noam Chomsky, *Pirates and Emperors*

It is not within the scope of this work to provide an exhaustive sociological analysis of international terrorism; however, it may be fruitful
to attempt to identify certain constants in the various subversive movements for the purpose of signalling 'terrorist flash points' in different
societies and perhaps provide an explanation of what happened recently in Italy and in the world of women.

One question is obligatory: is there a common element among the
forces of the macro system that, for example, in Czarist Russia, in
Germany and in Armenia, in some way facilitated the transformation
of a certain number of dissatisfied individuals in the middle- and upper-
bourgeois classes into a terrorist organisation? Before answering, let
us examine the following different situations in their broadest outlines.

The objectives of Noardonaja Wolja (1878–81) and of the Socialist
Revolutionary Russian Party that gave life to Russian terrorism were
the institution of democracy and the establishment of constitutional
rights, namely freedom of assembly and freedom of speech. The leaders
of the revolution were to be the Russian intellectual elite, while the
army was to be made up of the peasant population, which constituted
the majority of the Russian population and was still completely subservient to the great landowners.

As Vera Zasulič (1979) remembers in her memoirs, at that time, in
the absence of reliable information, any idea could find a home under
the grey mantle of the peasant who worked the land. Not only was it
possible, but for a certain segment of the intelligentsia, it was inevitable.
The invisible peasant played too important a role in the inner world of
the youth and in its plans for 'action' for the future. First of all, it was
necessary to formulate some hypotheses concerning the peasant. And
hypotheses were formulated in accordance with the subjective ideal of
man each person held. Thus, some believed the peasant was a born
revolutionary, ready to take up the hammer at a moment's notice. Others
believed he stood for altruism, equality and a number of other serene
virtues.

This enthusiasm is contrasted by the disappointment of another terrorist, Olga Ljubatovic who stated:

everyone sought the highest moral legitimization in the people, that of the 'rights of man', and not finding it in the Russian reality, within the masses called 'the people', they unsheathed their swords in the name of disfigured human nature reduced to a 'slave population'. True, there emerged from time to time from that people some powerful and commanding figures, but most of the time they slept in a deep slumber. An idealization accompanied by a deep sense of disappointment – that is the entire psychology of the 'heroic' period of our revolutionary history. (Zasulic *et al.*, 1979)

Thus, what characterised Russian terrorism in relation to the power it was bent on destroying was the idealisation of 'popular roots' that in reality did not exist and the desire for dedication to a single cause to deliver the oppressed, in this case the peasants, who never identified with the ideals of their 'liberators'. There was a great feeling of impotence before a power that, at the request for the most elementary democratic rights, responded with massacres in the streets, hangings and, in the best of cases, deportations to Siberia.

For its part, the *Rote Armee Fraction* (RAF) in Germany declared war against a State that was subservient to US imperialism, against the major industrial trusts and against the control of the levers of power by former Nazis. Proclaiming themselves the legitimate representatives of all the oppressed, both in Germany and in the Third World, they appealed to proletarian internationalism. The strategy of the RAF was synthesised by Ulrike Meinhof, who explained that to contest is to disapprove; to resist is to assume responsibility for eliminating what does not work. And counter-violence is the risk of violence itself. Thus, police brutality determines the method of action: paramilitary intervention by the police is answered with paramilitary methods.

But the marginalised never gathered round the terrorists of the RAF and the German population was never captivated by armed struggle. Even in the case of the RAF we can speak of an impossible war and an inevitable defeat, because the objectives were too grand for the meagre resources available; the terrorists lacked popular roots and their strategy – the terrorist threat – predictably produced the opposite of the desired effect, because it compelled the threatened State to tighten repression, which ended up undermining any support the terrorists may have had to begin with.

As for Italian terrorism, although it differed from Russian and German terrorism in many respects, it too may have been touched off by a feeling of helplessness before the power structure combined with the

lack of popular roots and the belief that the apparatus of the State had
been corrupted by power groups of Fascist inspiration. With the wisdom of hindsight, Mario Ferrandi recounts what may have drawn so
many young people like himself into the spiral of violence in that
particular historic period:

> What is worse is that we fell into the trap laid for us by the P2: the
> Piazza Fontana and the Italicus massacres were planned *ad hoc* in
> order to push a certain faction of the leftist movement towards ter-
> rorism and mobilise public opinion against it. We fell for it. . . . The
> Communist Party bears grave responsibility for this, since it taught
> us to ignore ethics, in the sense that it encouraged us to adopt a
> double standard in ethics, which leads to a tragic predicament. Un-
> der this double ethical standard, or rather no ethical standard, we
> believed that it was justifiable to kill those who bore grave respon-
> sibilities. (Appendices 4 and 10)

Identification of the political with the military is not new in the
history of the left and in the labour movement; indeed, in the Communist and Socialist tradition there was always room for a political concept that distinguished between violence on the part of the masses,
which was justified by the need to defend themselves or to overthrow
an oppressive regime, and that of individuals or small groups, not justified by those grander needs. Thus, when this concept of 'justifiable
violence of the masses' was combined, as was the case with many
militants, with the evangelical Utopia of a society redeemed from evil,
the result was an explosive mixture that gave the violence of 'proletarian squads' and of individual leaders the sense of rendering a final
accounting, of meting out unappealable justice.

The destiny of subversive movements that can count on vast popular support is different. Emblematic of this category is the ASALA
terrorist movement, which advocates the independence of the Armenian population from Turkish and former Soviet domination. This movement records its actions in the history of the resistance of the Armenian
population against powers guilty of forced conversions (the Armenians
are Catholic, the Russians Orthodox), pogroms and genocide. In order
to explain Armenian terrorism, Khachig Toloyan (1989) employed projective narration, that is, a form of expression that gives value to all
acts of resistance of the Armenian people in the past against enemy
invasion and confers a sacrificial meaning on death inflicted or suffered for this cause.

There are more wrongs and injustices than there are guerrilla, revolutionary or terrorist movements. But in this case there was, and there still is, a potent catalyst, that is, the combination of a vivid collective memory of injustice suffered and the paradigms traditionally ennobled by action – paradigms that pervade projective narration. To be an Armenian in the communities of the Middle East means, first of all, understanding one's daily experience of injustice in terms of family history and national narration, both of which are intimately related and, secondly, anticipating any confrontation with this injustice in terms of the narration of the preceding resistance.

The analogy with Italian terrorism consists of the fact that the Red Brigades and, to some extent, Prima Linea, also based their actions on traditional resistance to dictatorships and to foreign enemies allied with the dictatorship. Alberto Franceschini (1988) and Sergio Segio (Novelli, Tranfaglia, 1988) spoke of the importance of the narratives of ex-partisans in their decision to embrace armed struggle, the only remaining option, according to them, after the weapon of criticism revealed itself ineffective against a dictatorship masked as democracy. The continuity with the resistance was at times literal, in the sense that militants in some instances adopted the battle names of ex-partisan relatives or names that recalled extra-parliamentary groups or organisations or a Latin American guerrilla group. The ASALA movement is different in that the culture of continuity has become institutionalised by the Armenian people, to the point that it is found in childrens' textbooks, priests' sermons and in the poetry of intellectuals; in Italian terrorism continuity could only refer to a submerged culture that by that time was only surviving on tacit sympathy, symbols and songs – the sacred objects of a reality buried in the past. Furthermore, the Armenian culture values violent action as sacrificial action, even if this sacrifice has value as such for the privileged few (terrorists, popular heroes), while the people have the responsibility of creating these elected few and nurturing them with the mythology of the resistance. In Italy, on the other hand, a sort of subcultural anomy was created within the Communist subculture whose vague ideals encompassed a society free of exploitation, a paradise on earth (Silveria Russo in this regard recalls how much her revolutionary concept and that of her comrades, was merged with evangelical Utopia) and the means for realising all of this, which the militants believed could not be supplied by the democratic methods of the Communist Party.

4 CLICHÉS AND STEREOTYPES OF CRIMINOLOGICAL RESEARCH ON FEMALE DEVIANCE

> *Women may have happy ideas, taste, elegance, but they cannot attain to the ideal. The difference between men and women is like that between animals and plants. Men correspond to animals, while women correspond to plants because their development is more placid and the principle that underlies it is the rather vague unity of feeling.*

> G.W.F. Hegel, *Philosophy of Right*
> (Oxford: Oxford University Press, 1952)

> *Women are full of passion, Ananda; women are envious, Ananda; women are stupid, Ananda. That is the reason, Ananda, that is the cause, why women have no place in public assemblies, do not carry on business, and do not earn their living by any profession.*

> Dying Buddha to his disciple Ananda
> A. De Riencourt, *Women and Power in History*

It is revealing to compare the scarce quantity and quality of criminological research on women to that on men, which is extensive and well documented. Studies on female delinquency, in fact, have not produced a theoretical framework that goes much beyond the interpretations proposed by the early experts on delinquency.

Several writers have pointed to the narrow range of typifications of deviant women; as Feinman (1980) concluded, 'in the modern criminal justice system women are viewed according to attitudes that derive in large measure from classical Greece and Rome and medieval Europe. Both pagan mythology and Judeo-Christian theology present women with a dual nature, either as madonnas or as whores.'

In the dark ages commoners as well as the elite were concerned with witchcraft and its feminine representation; witch hunts resulted in the execution of several hundred witches, most of them women. Witchcraft was practically the only woman's crime for a long time. The logical relationship between being a woman and engaging in witchcraft was quite direct: witches are women, hence all women are potential witches. The image of the witch remains a potent symbol which can be easily conjured up – sometimes almost subliminally – as we have witnessed in recent cases such as the IRA's 'Evil Sisters'. As

Roland Barthes (1963) said: ' . . . if men condemn the witch, it is because they recognize her, because they project a part of themselves in her that is legitimate and intolerable at the same time'.

This image was taken from folklore and popular accounts and was uncritically adopted by 'scientific' criminologists such as Lombroso and Ferrero (1923) and Pollak (1961) as the basis of their theories about female crime, which have had a stigmatising effect as well as unfortunate consequences for the treatment of women offenders.

Next to the witch, the whore is the most potent image of female deviance, responsible for sexualising many, if not all, types of non-conforming female behaviour. Offences which have apparently nothing to do with sexuality are, when committed by women, transformed into expressions of female sexuality or the lack of it. Thus, we have the prostitute as sexual deviant, the kleptomaniac (the compulsive menopausal woman shoplifter), premenstrual violent woman and a number of other feminine stereotypes in which deviant behaviour, sexuality and illness are all enmeshed.

A remaining image which is even more damaging is that of the deviant woman as 'non-woman', or as masculine, unfeminine woman. Thus, women who engage in illegal activities considered traditionally the domain of men supposedly do so because they are, in essence, masculine. Women involved in politically deviant activities, the modern female terrorist in particular, have been portrayed as unisexed, unattractive and 'unnatural'. What distinguishes these 'classical' theorists is that they seek to rationalise and render intellectually acceptable a series of assumptions about women as biological beings and the consequences that flow therefrom for criminal behaviour. Women, in their view, are determined by their biology. Their hormones, their reproductive role, necessarily determine their emotionality, childishness, deviousness, etc. These traits, in turn, characterise female crime. If crime can be explained in biological terms, any adequate explanation has to explain why female, but not male, biology determines deviant behaviour. A partial answer to questions about sex differences in criminality is given by all these theorists: not only are women biologically distinct and uniquely behaviourally determined, their deviance is peculiarly sexual. Cesare Lombroso, in his famous treatise *The Delinquent Woman, the Prostitute and the Normal Woman* (1923), maintained that women criminals, unlike men, rarely show discernible signs of atavism since they are primitive to begin with and, hence, degenerative signs are confused with their underlying nature. The born female criminal (genetically closer to the male sex than to the female, inasmuch as she is bereft of the maternal instinct) possesses all the criminal traits of men combined with the worst traits of women, namely deceitfulness, cunning and resentment. Thus, female prostitution is either put on a par with ordinary male crime (Lombroso, 1903) or is diagnosed as the key symptom of the 'unadjusted' girl (Thomas, 1923). Prostitution is a typical manifestation of the criminal make-up of the female; if a prostitute commits particularly serious and repeated crimes, it is only due to her scarce intelligence, physical weakness or other limitations. Even apparently non-sexual crimes such as assault and theft are viewed as evidence of sexual repression. What is most important, however, is that far from being swamped by the modern criminological research tide, neo-Lombrosian studies of girl delinquents were still being carried out in the 1970s on the assumption that prostitution is evidence of individual psychopathology rather than a rational economic choice for women (McLeod, 1982). Indeed, as late as 1968 some theorists (Cowie *et al.*, 1968) were arguing that, though delinquency in boys may be primarily caused by social factors, delinquency in young women is mainly a matter of biology, specifically of non-fulfillment of gender role expectations (the judiciary in many countries continues to endorse this view).

The crude stereotyping of the 'sexual' nature of female crime and the exclusion of other factors (socio-economic, political, etc.) has not only been an obstacle to understanding female crime, but, on the practical level, has resulted in the unjust treatment of women as offenders and victims.

In other words, deviant men and women are viewed in markedly different ways. As a consequence, approaches that are considered archaic when applied to male delinquency still have currency in explaining female deviance. In fact, we still tend to attribute female deviant behaviour to particular biological or psychological traits that ignore the most recent interactionist and sociological findings. Dominant archetypes dating from the constitution of the patriarchal society, whose artful purpose was to create two counterposed blocks, still endure (Price and Solokoff, 1995). On the one hand, we have the male culture, with all that it entails, namely logos, cold rationality, active behaviour, selfcontrol, aggressivity, authoritativeness and the authoritarianism of the male who feels called upon to determine the destiny of the world, never doubting that he is the best, and, on the other, we have female biology, with all its stereotypes, to wit, behaviour governed by Eros, feelings that show through or are even flaunted, passive behaviour, surrender and a propensity to accept the judgment of males.

Women lacked ready initiative, the strength to lead ...

(Bruno Laronga, Chapter 4)

This is admittedly a portrait of manners and yet every individual belonging to one or the other blocks did his or her best to adhere to their own model, male or female, the penalty for non-conformity being marginalisation as different or alien (Giani Gallino, 1986).

Given this perspective, whenever social factors are taken into consideration they are deemed to apply on an individual level. The few scholars who studied the problem (Pollak, 1961; Heidenson, 1968) believe that it is not possible to evaluate female deviance using the same criteria used to evaluate male deviance because the norms imposed on women are different from those imposed on men. Feminine crime has traditionally been blamed on the failure of individual women to adapt to their supposedly natural biological and/or sociosexual destinies. As a result, in both criminological and lay explanations, criminal women have always been portrayed as being 'other': other than real women, other than real criminals and other than real prisoners (Carlen, 1991).

In other words, the essentially criminal woman does not exist. Women who break the law come from all sorts of backgrounds, (though, as in the case of male criminals, they tend to come from the lower socioeconomic strata), but once in the criminal justice system, women have to deal not with the reality, but with the myths that inform the criminal justice system and the prisons, namely that they are wicked, maladjusted or mentally ill.

In sum, it is not female criminality that is distinctive, but the defining and controlling apparatuses which they face and which limit their public and private behaviour in gender-related ways. The lack of interest in female criminality evident in orthodox criminology has also had the effect of rendering it insignificant in the eyes of the criminal justice system. Indeed, the official marginalisation of female deviance is justified by the apparently low level of crime among women.

More interesting is the approach that examines the relationship between the women's emancipation movement and quantitative and qualitative changes in female delinquency. According to Adler (1977), the change in women's condition that occurred during the 1960s, namely the masculinisation of women, coincided with the highest incidence of delinquency measured and a noticeable increase in violent crime. Thus, sexual equality was deemed responsible for the emergence of a new figure of the female delinquent, that is, a woman who joins gangs, drinks, joins scuffles and engages in crimes that are qualitatively different from the 'classical' ones like shoplifting.

A variation on this theory is that of the 'convergence' of roles, which posits the concomitant masculinisation of women and femininisation of men to explain the increasing similarity in criminal behaviour between the two sexes. This would seem especially so for middle-class adolescents who, unlike their lower-class cohorts, are socialised expecting more overlapping of feminine and masculine roles. In sum, the recurring theme in all the different theories that try to explain this phenomenon is to attribute the lower incidence of criminality among women to the lack of opportunity because of their sex. The fact is that female deviance does not constitute a social problem, because the violence and aggressivity manifested from time to time are not organised externally. A criminal career is still off-bounds to women. Weiss (1976) attempted to verify these different theories through an extensive study of female deviance. The author was able to establish the following relationships between the evolution of the female condition and criminality; (a) males are involved in more and more serious, delinquent behaviour; (b) the difference between male and female delinquency evidenced in anonymous surveys is less significant than that evidenced by police statistics on complaints and arrests and (c) with the exception of aggressive behaviour, still the domain of male delinquency, the types of deviant behaviour manifested by males and females are similar.

In essence, according to these studies the women's liberation movement had little impact on the phenomenon of female delinquency because the relationship between male and female delinquency has remained stable over time and the changes measured tend to disprove the theories. And, to conclude, female delinquency should be interpreted in light of women's position in society and of the different opportunities they have. Yet it is an uncontrovertible fact that the process of socialisation of males and females still under way in many countries today is different. Traditionally the place of primary socialisation for both sexes was the family; but whereas the prospective role of the man extends to the whole of society in which he will be integrated and will develop his own identity, a woman's relationship to society, traditionally speaking, is not direct, but mediated through the family. A man moves on the public scene and his behaviour is controlled by the rules and laws that govern it, and those are the rules he breaks in the case of deviant behaviour. A woman's backdrop is the family and the sexual sphere. It follows, therefore, that female deviant behaviour involves breaking the specific rules governing her world.

Table 2.1   The ideal roles of men and women in the family

Country	Both have a demanding job and share roles equally	The wife has a less demanding job and does more of the housework	Husband has the job and the wife stays at home
Belgium	34	30	25
Denmark	53	26	12
Germany	26	34	32
Greece	43	28	23
France	45	29	24
Ireland	34	20	39
Italy	42	31	25
Luxembourg	20	30	39
The Netherlands	43	28	23
Portugal	43	24	25
Spain	47	19	28
UK	48	31	18

Notes: The results are given in percentages.

Source: Eurobarometer 1987: Public Opinion in the European Community (published by the European Commission).

These role expectations ensure that girls learn passive strategies early on and, in some cases, even self-destructive ones to resolve conflicts rather than resort to violent manifestations of deviance, for which their specific socialisation has not trained them. It is also clear that role changes that have come about in the female world in recent decades have, at least in some countries, seriously upset this traditional scheme of assumption of roles. In the United States there seems to be substantial agreement on the part of experts that qualitative changes are under way in female juvenile delinquency, that is, a progression from classical female deviance (vagabondage, running away from home, prostitution, shoplifting, child abuse, etc.) to more serious deviance, such as burglaries, homicides, robberies and joining gangs – not in the traditional role of the gang leader's moll, but as active protagonists in armed robbery, extortion and the like. A quantitative change was documented as well. According to the United Nation Report of the Secretary-General 22 September 1977 (A/32/199) the world crime situation indicates that the overall rate for the years 1970–5 was approximately 900 offenders per 100,000 population and that the offenders rate increased steadily by 2% annually. For the period considered, the total increase has thus been approximately 15%. For adult offenders, the male rate was ten times greater than that for females. For juvenile offenders, the male rate was five times greater that that for females. In developing countries the overall rate of criminal offenders for the period 1970–5 was approximately 800 per 100,000 population. The number of offenders increased at an annual rate of approximately 2.5%. The rate of increase for females was 30% higher than that for males. For adult offenders, the rate for males was twelve times greater than that for females and for juvenile offenders, the rate for males was eight times greater than that of females. Crime in developed countries was 1,000 per 100,000 population and the number of offenders has increased steadily at an annual rate of 1%. The rate of female offenders has increased 50% more rapidly that that of the male. The overwhelming proportion of adult offenders were males, with a rate eight times that for females. For juvenile offenders, the rate for males was five times greater than for females.

An extraordinary case was reported in Iran, in 1981, involving the execution by firing squad of a group of young people involved in anti-government activities in which the percentage of women was very high: 30 of the 81 people executed were women.

5   GENDER AND THE CRIMINAL JUSTICE SYSTEM

> *Nature has determined woman's destiny through beauty, charm and sweetness . . . in youth an adored darling, in mature years a loved wife.*
>
> Freud (in Jones, *The Life and Works of Sigmund Freud*)

In a sociolegal study on the condition of German women, Oekinghaus (1925) concluded that women were in an ambiguous and untenable position in relation to modern culture, for this culture placed demands on them which they could not meet and engendered feelings of insufficiency and helplessness and embroiled them in situations they could not untangle – and all that despite the fact that women rejected such culture.

When we examine the legal apparatus designed to deal with crime and criminals, we clearly see how difficult it is for women to fit into its categories and its correctional system. Women, who have traditionally been at a disadvantage before the law, are too easily assimilated into so-called problem groups and socially marginal categories.

A long-term social trend has been under way to grant legal standing to more and more classes of people with the consequence that previously unrecognised plaintiffs have begun to have a say under the law as holders of rights. Thus, women, children, the elderly, the handicapped, the ill, homosexuals and even animals are now granted certain legal rights. At the national and international levels, constitutional and statutory guarantees have been put into effect to create and defend the *ad hoc* legal identities of these new groupings. In other words, women, the majority of mankind, are a 'socially marginal group' that have finally been accorded legal status thanks to a long overdue change in the legal system.

Criminal law has undoubtedly undergone radical change, but, by and large, it continues to be governed by a male perspective. The need to control women and children is expressed explicitly in criminal law. In many countries women are still considered more or less as chattels owned by their husbands and, accordingly, the law defines rape as a property offence. The same considerations apply with respect to adultery, which is often defined as an essentially feminine crime, and to various traditional practices of female mutilation. In many cultures female sexuality is associated with danger and evil, as the role of the good woman is that of childbearer. There are often sharp distinctions between 'respectable' and 'bad' women, sexual experience being the mark of the latter. Like procreation, sexuality is not an individually determined matter. The same historical forces that govern parenthood act upon sexual choices and female sexuality has been legally and socially narrowed to acceptable channels of heterosexual monogamy. Women are viewed as passive, emotional, dependent, inferior as well as inciting: they live and work under the authority of the husband (UN A/CONF. 121/16/1985).

According to a UN report by the Commission on Human Rights (E/CN.4/1986/42 ECOSOC), 'the Working Group referred to various traditional practices such as female circumcision, other forms of mutilation (facial scarification), forced feeding of women, various taboos or practices which prevent women from controlling their fertility etc.' Female circumcision is a particularly loathsome practice still carried out in at least 28 African countries that jeopardises the health of approximately 75 million women and children. 'These practices', states the UN report, 'generally derive from the role and status of women in society. In most cases, the purpose of the various practices is to control female sexuality and conserve the monogamic status of women. Infibulation is thus practiced not only on young girls in order to guarantee their virginity, but also on widows, divorcees, and married women in the event of a prolonged absence of their husbands.'

The reasons put forward to justify female circumcision in the sample studied in the report are as follows.

Tradition	54.2%
Religion	18.6%
Facility of sexual relations	4.8%
Diminution of women's sensitivity	27.5%
Without opinion but in favour	7.5%

As Mannheim (1965) explained, hitherto female crime has, for all practical purposes, been dealt with almost exclusively by men in their various capacities as legislators, judges and policemen and this could not fail to create a one-sided picture. The classical subject of criminal law is the adult competent individual, abstracted from his context, defined in Italian law as a person capable of understanding and volition. Yet this adult competent individual happens to be male; thus the criteria for competency are historically male oriented.

Male patterns of thought and evaluation are still considered 'human' by definition. Women, minors and the mentally ill have traditionally been exceptions and treated as such, either by not being processed through the criminal justice system or by being processed through it in a different way. Holding down female crime and doling out shorter prison sentences in the event of convictions have been paid for by diminished legal safeguards, greater arbitrariness, judicial paternalism and generally being subjected to other types of social control (Pitch, 1992).

In sum, therefore, following the trend set by social theories of deviance that continue to emphasise gender roles even though the female part of the continuum was never studied, the criminal justice system persists in ignoring at least half of the population.

From the perspective of sociological research on female criminality, the reason why legislation pertaining to women offenders often misses the target may be that their behaviour is viewed as a deviation from dominant male norms; female criminality is therefore defined by sociologists as a subculture.

Psychologists have found sex differences in their studies from the moment they started doing empirical research. But since it is difficult to avoid value judgement and there is a tendency to adopt one measure for all even though such a measure is admittedly derived from men's interpretations of research data on males, psychologists have tended to regard male behaviour as the 'norm' and female behavior as a deviation from that norm (Gilligan, 1982).

But as soon as gender is correlated with other social factors such as age, social class and level of education, this leads to varied and at times contradictory results and no explanation of these differences has proved satisfactory. Most studies show differences in the attitudes of men and women towards the law and the criminal justice system. However, remarkably few of the differences found in one set of studies remain unchallenged in another. And even the differences established disappear when other social characteristics are added to the mix. As Kutchinsky (1973) stresses, all gender-specific differences become invalid in younger age groups due to increasing urbanisation and higher standards of living and education. A theory based simply on roles or so-called sex characterisation can no longer be offered impartially and uncritically as an explanation.

International research (Gerhard, 1993) has shown great disparity and diversity in the level of knowledge about the law and attitudes toward the law in different populations. Women seem to have 'deficient' knowledge of, and a 'weak' interest in, the law, but their opposition to legal norms and judgements does not imply alienation from the legal system in general, but only from male-centred law. And since women's sense of justice differs in many respects from that of men, there should be a justice system that respects such differences. In a more recent empirical study (Blankenburg, 1982) gender-specific analysis of the data showed that no significant differences could be ascertained between men and women in the overall sample. Instead, class-specific variables such as background, education and profession rather than gender were shown to influence legal awareness of women to a greater extent.

Questions concerning gender have become increasingly significant in the field of sociolegal research; indeed, gender has become an important variable in many research projects. Perhaps the most important single contribution made by modern sociologists to the study of deviance has been their emphasis on the need to study public descriptions of, and social reactions to, deviant behaviour. The importance of the media and the related public reaction to patterns of crime and deviance is well established. What then of deviant women? Are the images presented of them very different from those of men? Are public reactions different and, if so, what consequences do these differences have?

In fact, the popular media do seem captivated by deviant women. Female crime has attracted great interest in notorious figures such as Ulrike Meinhof, Patty Hearst and Italian women terrorists. Women involved in murder cases have attracted more than their share of attention, but so have women involved in spying, terrorism and sex scandals. As a result, certain categories of female criminal behaviour are over-represented in the media and they appear to attract more interest than do men in such cases.

To break out of both the gender trap and the misleading 'masculine–feminine' dilemma, theorists should abandon stable referents for these categories and adopt the assumption that social constructs concerning gender vary both across and within societies and that they have heterogeneous effects, as they combine with other forms of differentiation, in particular as they combine with the differential effects of culture, religious background, race, class, etc.

Just as it is important to learn about the criminal justice system of others, there is little doubt that the comparative approach leads to a better understanding of our own system as well as of the interdependence between law and other social phenomena. The criminal justice system is actually an instrument of social control and it is thus influenced by and influences social life in numerous ways. In fact, the cultural settings within which the systems operate produce very different outputs. As a result, one may be easily misled into assuming that two institutions perform the same function in different countries because they bear the same name, or that the fact of sharing the same name automatically entails similar features, interpretation, treatment, etc., in different criminal systems.

Although procedures and institutions used in one culture may not develop in the same manner in another environment, often elements can be shifted and knowledge of the experience of others can point to actions that should be followed or avoided.

Theories of gender should be contextual and attuned to the cultural specificity of different societies and periods. According to some authors (Petersen, 1992), one of the tasks feminists face in understanding the law in post-modern society is to define a common starting point for women in different situations to help bridge cross-class and cross-cultural experiences.

6 THE FIRST UNITED NATIONS SURVEY ON THE SITUATION OF WOMEN AND THE ADMINISTRATION OF CRIMINAL JUSTICE SYSTEMS, 1970–83

In 1983 the UN Secretariat conducted the First United Nations Survey on Women and the Administration of Criminal Justice Systems. This survey is unique and valuable because, as stated in the report 'for the first time ever, world-wide data and information have been gathered on a major social issue that has been virtually neglected: women in criminal justice'. This survey of criminal justice systems encompassed both adult and juvenile segments separately. Respondents were asked to reflect on the situation of both adult and juvenile female offenders whenever possible. An open-ended format questionnaire which allowed considerable latitude in the responses was distributed to the network of 250 government-appointed national correspondents in the field of crime prevention and control. The questionnaire focused on the following:

(a) female criminality and delinquency;

(b) prevention strategies;

(c) the differential treatment and handling of females while in criminal justice custody;

(d) the role and status of women in the administration of criminal justice.

The Questionnaire

The questionnaire is divided into two sections.

Section I (three questions) concerns 'Women as Practitioners and Administrators in Criminal Justice'. Section II concerns 'Women as Offenders' and asks the following questions on female delinquency and criminality.

4. In general terms, what has been the nature and extent of female delinquency and criminality since 1970?

5. Since 1970, has there been a considerable involvement of females in crimes of violence? If possible specify age groups.

6. If there has been a great or greater involvement of females in

crimes of violence during this period, what countermeasures have been or are being taken by the relevant authorities to cope with this situation?

7. Has there been any change in the extent and seriousness of drug- and alcohol-related female delinquency and criminality, since 1970, according to the police and/or other official records? If so, please give details.

8. (a) Please indicate the proportion of recorded female delinquency and criminality, relative to the total for all persons, since 1970, if possible.

   (b) Since 1970, which types of crimes have been committed more frequently than others by female offenders?

   (c) What significant changes have occurred in the commission of those crimes by females since 1970?

9. (a) Which factors (socioeconomic, cultural, demographic, etc.) are considered as contributing to stability or any observed changes in the dimensions of female delinquency and criminality, as indicated in the previous answer?

   (b) Has there been any evidence that the increase in opportunities for females has affected, in any way, the profile of the female offender?

10. Have those factors, identified as affecting female crime in some way, been taken into account in policy by the relevant authorities?

The Secretariat received reports from the following 53 countries:

Argentina	Central Africa Republic
Australia	Chile
Victoria	Columbia
Tasmania	Costa Rica
Austria	Cyprus
Bahrain	Czechoslovakia
Bangladesh	Denmark
Barbados	Ecuador
Belgium	Finland
Belize	France
Bolivia	Germany Federal Republic
Botswana	Greece
Canada	India

Ireland
Israel
Italy
Japan
Kenya
Libyan Arab Jamahiriya
Malaysia
Mauritania
Morocco
New Zealand
Nigeria
Norway
Oman
Panama
Papua New Guinea
Philippines
Poland

Qatar
Rwanda
Senegal
Seychelles
Spain
Sweden
Switzerland
United Arab Emirates
United Kingdom of Great Britain
   and Northern Ireland
England and Wales
Northern Ireland
Scotland
Venezuela
Yugoslavia
Zambia

The percentage by region is as follows: North America and Western Europe (77%); Eastern Europe (60%); Asia and the Pacific (53%); Latin America and the Caribbean (50%); Western Asia (44%); and Africa (41%).

Late reports from Brazil, Indonesia, Portugal, the Republic of Korea, Saint Vincent and the Grenadines, Sudan, Surinam and Togo were of better quality and Portugal and Korea made available data containing comprehensive analyses and were accompanied by extensive supporting documentation.

Given the variation in quality, extent and completeness of the responses to the questionnaire, fundamental difficulties of content analysis were encountered. As stated in the report, the analysis reflects a trade-off between the preservation of detail, on the one hand and two key considerations in survey research methodology, reliability and comparability, on the other.

Analysis of trends and presentation of survey data were made on the basis of the overall situation and, where possible, on the basis of categorisation by region (on the basis of geographical proximity and/ or cultural similarity) and stage of development (developed $N = 25$, developing $N = 27$, and least developed $N = 4$).

Owing to the limitations of unstructured questionnaires and varying response styles, the findings of the survey require great caution in their generalisation beyond the time frame under discussion (1970–82) or the countries analysed. Additional limitations are required regarding comparisons by regional and developmental groupings. Indeed, the marked disparity observed both in terms of response rates and in terms of absolute numbers of responding countries in each region, precluded the application of the usual tests of statistical significance.

The results obtained can be summarised as follows:

1. For the most part, the amount of female crime during the period 1970–82 shows a constant increase; according to survey data, 52.5% of the responding countries reported an overall increase in the incidence of female criminality, 15% reported a decline and 32.5% reported no change (Figure 2.1).

2. The gap between male and female crime figures for certain offences is beginning to narrow.

3. Some developed countries indicated that female crime rates, particularly for juveniles, rose faster than male crime rates over the period (30% in developing countries and 50% in developed countries). This finding was also reported by a number of the developed countries at the Fifth Congress of the United Nations held in 1975.

4. Family-related offences, such as infanticide, child abuse, murder of the spouse, adultery, abortion, welfare fraud as well as prostitution and other moral offences were cited as conventional female crimes in many countries and constituted the majority of female crimes around the world.

5. In many countries serious concern was expressed with regard to what appeared to be an increasing female involvement in drug trafficking, both domestically and on an international scale.

6. The increasing involvement of females, particularly among younger women, in violent crime, large-scale disturbances and rioting, attacks on public and private property, gang and terrorist activities was reported as a serious development in some countries. In fact, as stated in the Secretary-General's report, women as armed robbers and terrorists have become the subject of scientific inquiry over the past decade. Approximately one country in three reported an increase in the incidence of female involvement in violent crime, few reported a decrease and approximately one-quarter reported that, during the time period, female involve-

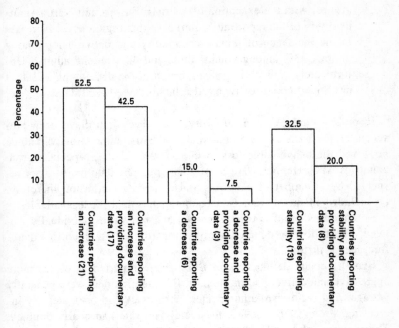

Figure 2.1 Changes in the incidence of female criminality and delinquency, 1970–82 (N = 40)

ment in crimes of violence had remained unchanged. But it is important to emphasise that approximately 38% of the countries reported that there were no data available concerning the actual extent of female involvement in violent crime.

7. As regards the reported changes, there was no substantial variation by region or by group at different levels of development (the percentage of countries reporting increases were within the range of 33–45% for all regions, except for Western Asia which reported no increase). The increases seemed most pronounced in countries of North America and Western Europe. Increases were reported by 50% of the least developed, 40% of the developed and 33.3% of the developing countries. Decreases were reported by 16% of the developed, 7.4% of the developing and 0% in the least developed countries.

8. According to the survey data, 56% of countries reported no significant variation in female criminal involvement among age

groups, with the exception of Western Europe and North America (58% of the reporting countries of that region noted increases in the incidence of female criminality and delinquency among minors, 53% among young adults and 42% among adults). Unfortunately, a much larger proportion of the developing and least developed countries reported a lack of age-based data.

In order to achieve comparability, the survey data have been presented on the basis of the global situation. This methodological choice provoked the unavoidable loss of considerable detail, especially from countries whose replies were most complete. The dateline was not respected by a number of countries and their data could not, therefore, be included in the survey. Consequently, the data made available by these countries could not be processed and remained individually isolated. The following detailed analysis regarding these countries therefore seems justified.

Brazil: female delinquents in Brazil were reported to be far more aggressive and active than in the past. Female offenders were generally younger and recidivism among female criminals had been steadily increasing. From 1976 to 1982, the recidivism rate had nearly doubled. The majority of female offenders (67%) were between the age of 18 and 29 years. Crimes committed most frequently were theft and robbery (52%), drug trafficking and drug abuse (20%) and crimes against the person (16%). Robbery accompanied by violence committed by females constituted 7% of the total number of robberies.

Portugal: from 1970 to 1980 the proportion of female crime of the total was reportedly 12–13%. With regard to violent crime, the female crime rate remained stable. Available data on drug- and alcohol-related crime and delinquency did not differentiate between females and males. The most frequent crimes committed by women were assault, injury against public officials, calumny and defamation. The decline in the number of incarcerated females must be attributed to changes in penal and procedural policy rather than to a decrease in female criminality.

Republic of Korea: female criminality was reported to have been 'steeply increasing' during the period 1970–82. The most prevalent female crime (25% of total female crime) involved property and a significant increase in crimes involving morality was reported owing to changing patterns of sexual behaviour that contravened customs. The proportion of female to male offenders and delinquents remained relatively constant. This was explained by the fact that the process of rapid development and the equalisation of opportunities for women had reached a stage of relative stability. The majority of female offenders (70%) were between the ages of 26 and 50 years, were poor and married, and had not completed middle school.

Indonesia: a slight overall increase in female criminality since 1970 was reported and police reports indicated that the types of crimes committed by women had become more complex. Female offenders were most often between 18 and 25 years of age. There was a significant increase in the extent and seriousness of drug- and alcohol-related female delinquency. This was viewed as the result of illegal alcoholic beverages being made available to school-children by street vendors.

According to the Indonesian Central Bureau of Statistics, female criminality constituted 3.3% of the total crime rate in 1980 and 3.8% in 1981. The crimes committed more frequently by women than men were fraud and theft, illegal abortion and infanticide.

The report concluded that cultural and demographic factors contributed to the pattern of female delinquency and criminality observed from 1970 to 1982. In particular, the report concluded that changing attitudes and an increase in opportunities for females had resulted in a considerable change in the profile of the female offender. Female offenders had been treated more leniently than male offenders and they had often been sent back to their families to try to resolve conflicts. It had been the practice of law enforcement officers to try to settle cases of female criminality outside the court room.

Saint Vincent and the Grenadines: the rate of female crime was reported to have remained stable and without significant change during the reporting period. No change was reported in drug- and alcohol-related female delinquency and criminality. There was no significant increase in female involvement in crimes of violence; however, the crimes most frequently committed by women were said to be assaults and bodily harm. Females were more likely to be fined for an offence than to receive a prison sentence.

Surinam: theft, assault, prostitution and drug crimes were reported to constitute the largest portion of female criminality.

There was a slight increase overall and, specifically, during 1979–82, there was greater involvement of females in crimes of violence and drug- and alcohol-related offences. The proportion of recorded female crime and delinquency relative to the total since 1970 did not exceed 10% and did not fall below 4%. Drug offences had become the most frequently recorded offences. There was evidence that increases in opportunities for females had affected the profile of the female offender, contributing to the change in the dimensions of female criminality and delinquency.

There had been a significant increase in the number of incarcerated female offenders in proportion to the total prison population. Females were accorded 'softer' treatment. There were certain cultural beliefs that women are less dangerous than males. The only basis for differential treatment was culturally defined and determined.

Togo: the nature and frequency of female delinquency in Togo was reported as being very limited and usually settled outside the court system. Cases that reached the criminal justice system included crimes such as abortion, fraud, infanticide, abandonment and adultery (abortion and adultery are no longer criminal offences in Togo).

Poor economic conditions associated with underdevelopment were cited as factors that contributed to the occurrence of female crime against children. Drug- and alcohol-related offences had not been a problem in Togo during the reporting period.

Differential treatment of female offenders was not legally grounded, but based on societal values and traditions which resulted in the accordance of favourable treatment to females. They were granted judicial pardons, fines and suspended sentences as alternatives to imprisonment more frequently than the men were.

7 THE CHIVALRY FACTOR: MYTH AND REALITY

The survey data suggest that there is a progressive shift in the official response to female deviance away from the 'chivalrous leniency' that has traditionally characterised official reaction to female criminality (Hecht Schafran, 1995). This erosion, as the UN report underlines, appears particularly pronounced when female offenders do not commit traditionally female crimes. But very little is understood of the relationship between female criminality and the behaviour of criminal justice systems. Girls and women do undoubtedly have lower recorded crime rates. Female crime has therefore had a low public profile.

The role played by criminal justice agencies – the police, the courts, the prisons, etc. – in the labelling and shaping of the 'female crime problem' has been underestimated. Data on the treatment of female offenders at each stage of the criminal justice process have consistently been less complete than data on the incidence of female criminality (which has been less than adequate). Given the paucity of data (in UN surveys, between 41 and 61% of responding countries indicate a lack of data), it is not surprising that prevailing assertions that women are treated more leniently than men have been accepted at face value for so many years.

Evidence of leniency and preferential treatment in dealing with female offenders is generally apparent when considering aggregate data on criminal justice processing. Such data indicate that generally less severe sanctions are being imposed on women; data from a number of countries indicate a somewhat more frequent use of diversionary sanctions and higher rates of suspended sentences. The statements of some reporting countries are self-explanatory.

Sudan: since women were placed under the protection of men, action by relevant authorities to deal with problems of female crime were often neglected. Given women's status in society, they were accorded more lenient treatment as offenders than men in the criminal justice system. In light of their traditions, social rather than legal disciplinary sanctions were often taken against female offenders to protect them from shame and dishonour that would be caused by a trial, detention or imprisonment.

As **Japan** observed: 'it is undeniable that female offenders get more lenient dispositions. . . . However, this should not be understood to suggest that there is differential treatment of female offenders, but that the nature and seriousness of offenses committed by women, the criminal record of female offenders and other relevant factors are reflected in the differences in the statistical figures.'

In fact, while females in some countries are accorded preferential treatment and special handling in many cases, in others they are subject to harsher measures, particularly in the case of juveniles, and for certain types of crime and acts of delinquency (e.g., moral, status offences), which may be viewed as serious infractions of expected behavioural roles or moral precepts (Report of the Secretary-General E.AC.57/1984/15). In some countries women are placed in mental institutions, jails or prisons for sexual misconduct and young females can be institutionalised for social misconduct or even misbehaviour at home.

But with few exceptions, the international data indicate a clear trend toward the imprisonment of women (40% of countries reporting increases) and in many societies females in conflict with the law are being accorded less leniency than a decade ago.

8   REPORTED CAUSES OF FEMALE CRIME

Most reporting correspondents provide an analysis of the factors contributing, in their view, to observable changes in the nature and extent
of female criminality and delinquency. Growth in female crime rates
has been linked to the emancipation of women for more than a century (Pike, 1876; Bishop, 1931; Pollak, 1961). In examining the de-
velopments in sex-role theory and crime Bertrand (1969) attempted to
show, on an international basis, how women's self-perception, cultural
stereotypes of female roles, penal codes and female emancipation can
all be related. Thus, she argued that female crime rates vary with the
degree of women's involvement with the home and children, and that
where women have well-established civil rights, penal codes are not
discriminatory. Her hypotheses, however, were not supported by her
empirical studies. In any case, even if women are not in fact conform-
ing to stereotypes, the chances are that their behaviour will be so defined by social agencies. Involvement in crime must be the outcome
of a variety of social, economic and other pressures and there are no *a
priori* reasons for believing that female crime should be different from
male crime; indeed it is clear that women can and do emulate men in
committing all types of crime.

As Adler (1977) concludes: 'Just as women are demanding equal
opportunity in fields of legitimate endeavour, a number of determined
women are forcing their way into the world of major crime.' Carlen
(1991) shares the same view: 'As women acquire the same legal rights
as men they will cast off their chains . . . and commit crimes like men.

All countries responding to the UN survey emphasised the relationships between female criminality and developmental factors – including trends toward emancipation and equal rights and opportunities.

Whether countries reported an increase, decrease or stability in the
incidence of female criminality and delinquency, most attributed the
change or lack of change to the socio-economic status of women.

Some responding countries reported that the increase was due to
increasing opportunities and changing social roles, others reported that
increasing female crime rates were due to a lack of socio-economic
opportunities and increasing marginalisation of women, other countries
reported that the decrease was due to increasing opportunities and changing life styles and still others reported stability and attributed this to
the equalisation of opportunities for women.

According to the report from **Brazil**, women's independence has greatly
influenced the increased incidence of female crime – particularly violent crime. Other factors contributing to the increase in female criminality,

according to the Brazilian report, included population growth, rapid changes in values and customs and 'women's liberation'. Factors that contributed to channelling social aggression into female crime were especially evident in the case of female juvenile offenders.

According to the report from **Portugal**, the profile of the female offender was affected by the new social status of women achieved in 1974.

Saint Vincent and the Grenadines cited lack of parental care, unstable family life, unemployment, underemployment and overcrowding as factors contributing to the occurrence of female delinquency.

According to the report from **Sudan**, social restraint played a major role in deterring women from involvement in crime. Men were entrusted with the responsibility for women's well-being and protection from crime. The slight increase in the incidence of female criminality was attributed to the fact that women had recently been more exposed to crime-producing influences as a result of their increased participation in work outside the home.

Spain: 'Because of the integration of women into social and professional life, female delinquency is tending to become more like male delinquency, not only as regards the kinds of offenses committed, but also the degree of participation in the offenses. . . . Females are emancipated earlier from the family and join gangs . . . as members of the group or in more active roles, even as a leaders. . . . A further consequence of the integration of women into social life is their increasing involvement in terrorist groups.'

Colombia: 'Economic necessity was mainly responsible for leading women into criminal activities; this is seen from their considerable involvement in drug trafficking and their active participation in corruption and fraud. . . . Access to (different) fields has perhaps provided women with further possibilities for overcoming economic difficulties. . . . Statistics show that, as opportunities for women increase, "new" forms of offenses appear. . . . The involvement of women in offenses of a political nature goes hand in hand with their increased access to higher education, which has made them aware of the degree of oppression and inequality they have been subjected to both on the personal and on the social level.'

According to the report from **Nigeria**, 'the incidence of delinquency and criminality among females would have been higher if there had not been an increase in opportunities for them'.

Federal Republic of Germany: 'women have fewer chances to commit offenses . . . due to their sex role and the stronger social controls exercised [over them] in the process of socialization. . . . To explain the increase in female criminality, reference is made . . . to the greater participation of women in gainful employment and, generally, to the process of female emancipation . . . described as a process of de-differentiation of the roles played by the sexes.'

Canada: 'It is difficult to determine what portion of the increase is due to an increase in female criminality and what portion is due to changes in the criminal justice system's response to female offenders. It may be that the women' movement has spurred police and victims to lay charges against females more frequently than before and, in effect, to treat female suspects as they would their male counterparts.'

Bangladesh: 'The impact of the transition from an agriculture-based society to a developing society on female criminality and delinquency is beginning to be felt, but the problem has not yet taken on acute form.'

It seems clear that the process of causal attribution of female criminality is still dominated by stereotypes and characterised by contradictions and inconsistencies which affect the premise itself, namely that female crime is under-reported. Scepticism about both the validity and reliability of criminal statistics is now more or less universal; the annual British Criminal Statistics publication stresses the limitations of the data it presents (Home Office, 1983a). Two principal features limit the official recording of crime: the iceberg effect (the tip of the iceberg is visible while there are many offences which go unobserved, unreported and unrecorded) and the dark figure (uncleared crimes about which very little detail is available such as age, sex or social characteristics of the perpetrator).

There are also several factors which may have a particular impact on the recording of female criminality. The only certain data on the sex of offenders comes either from police records or the courts; in other words, from a very select sample of people and events.

A further uncertainty lies in the extent of possible bias in reporting and recording offences by girls and women; all we can say is that the propensity to report women's crimes may differ from the propensity to report those of men, but to what degree we cannot say.

9 FEMALE POLITICAL DEVIANCE

> *And, what's more, that ruin was visited on the Romans because of a woman, a fact that caused them great shame.*
>
> D. Cassius, *Historia Augusta*

We can safely say that women involved in armed subversion do not fit the stereotype of women who 'deviate' because they are led astray by men or to become a gang leader's moll, although some women terrorists did conform to this stereotype. Francesca Mambro set herself the task of making life more serene and liveable for neo-fascist fugitives (interview by S. Zavoli, 1990). But Giulia Borelli (Malagutti, 1987) rejects the *pasionaria* label given by the press to Mambro; Tosi did not appreciate the fact that her male comrades referred to the women as 'angels of the copying machine' (Malagutti, 1987); Grazia Grena went underground in order to be close to her fugitive comrades and caused a rupture in her family by doing so (Passerini, 1988); Carmen De Stefano exploited her companion to become a regular militant in the Red Brigades (Passerini, 1988); Renata Chiari remained obdurately non-cooperative while her husband became a 'super penitent' of the Walter Alasia column; Silveria Russo and Susanna Ronconi decided, against the opinion of the men, to form a female commando squad to strike an over-zealous female prison guard in the Turin penitentiary (see Appendix 7); and Mara Cagol decided, against the opinion of many of her comrades, to help her husband, Renato Curcio, escape from the Monferrato jail (Franceschini, 1988).

As the opinion of the Court of Assizes points out, most of the outstanding members of the Walter Alasia Column – Daniela Figini, Ada Negroni, Betti Pasqua Aurora, Renata Chiari and Vita Casavola – undertook at considerable risk to themselves to plan and execute a breakout for comrades held in the San Vittore jail. As Mara Aldrovandi noted in response to query no. 8 of the questionnaire ('There were times when I felt less attached to armed struggle . . .'), the breakouts were a higher priority for the women than for the men in hiding, because the men feared a loss of personal power if a leader in the movement were to escape from prison (see Appendix 2). The court's opinion in the Walter Alasia Column case also points out that the national command of the Red Brigades sent a woman, Barbara Balzerani, with Moretti to reconstruct the Walter Alasia Column, which had been decimated by the 1979 arrests; and her disagreement with another woman, Betti Pasqua Aurora, was the reason Balzerani returned to Rome; and later Ms Zaccheo was able to make her agenda for the Walter Alasia Column, to wit its focus on the 'centrality' of the working class, prevail over the national platform of the Red Brigades, which focused on attacking the heart of the State. And Ms Ronconi remained in Prima Linea while the man she loved, Segio Sergio, left the organisation to found the small Communist Nuclei.

Ms Ronconi's recollection of the events is as follows (Passerini, 1988):

> In that year (1982), there was a situation in which the famous 'COLP' were a kind of 'combattant matriarchy,' because there was a majority of women from a numerical standpoint, perhaps because of the way the arrests occurred, and some of us were comrades with the greatest seniority, and thus, in effect, the leadership of the group was composed of four women ... they held the group together, kept everyone from going berserk, from losing themselves. And this is something for which S. and his group criticized us even back then, that it was a mistake not to send most of the militants to France. Because as a result many militants had to be supported ... it was just like the burden of a large family ... the women were accused of being too maternal, of sticking to the idea that, as long as we're together, as long as we have a relationship between ourselves, we can make it. This is the kind of illusion, of thinking, we had.

From the statements cited earlier, made during a seminar conducted by Luisa Passerini and Bianca Guidetti Serra with former terrorists incarcerated in the 'Vallette' prison, as well as from our own interviews it is apparent that some of the women took part in the self-awareness groups of the feminist movement. Susanna Ronconi, Silveria Russo, Giulia Borelli, Carmen De Stefano, Nadia Mantovani and Grazia Grena were all active in the feminist movement for a short period and all felt that it was 'too constricting'. In the end they all left because they became impatient with the endless discussions that never resulted in action. The 'endless discussions' of the feminist self-awareness groups made it clear that the innermost history of women was not written with the tales of Ulysses, nor Prometheus, in mind, as their centuries-old identity does not emphasize challenge, measuring oneself, rushing towards horizons all the more fascinating because difficult to attain. Women, according to Birgit Brock-Utne (1989), are instead inherently conservative in their physiological need to care for human needs, and only in this expressive solicitude, which is not instrumental, can they find the strength to fight against a capitalistic system that looks to profits rather than needs.

We find confirmation of this evaluation in philosopher Umberto Galimberti's (1989) *Il Gioco Delle Opinioni*, to which we certainly cannot attribute feminist sympathies. In his rather hermetic language he states that women, inasmuch as they are 'laboratories of procreation', do not possess culture, only 'care' that is repeated in the rhythm of insignificance, because it is always the same thing, repeated in cyclical sameness. Men, on the other hand, inasmuch as they are the 'laboratories of production', are naturally prone to look up to the sky, that is, to ideas cleansed of matter.

If we transpose this argument into the framework of our discussion we would say that a woman is by her very nature extraneous to palingenetic and eschatological perspectives precisely because these cannot take into consideration what is specifically feminine, to wit, acts of daily conservation; not action aimed at achieving future goals, but at structuring a microsocial order as free as possible from tensions and potential threats (Ambroset, 1984).

But the feminists started from this specifically feminine trait and made 'care' the model of a 'different culture', and on the basis of this model demanded an equality that was not the simple opportunity for women to do everything men do, assuming that any change in the patriarchal society requires greater self-awareness on the part of women (whereby, for example, abnegation becomes acceptable as a life value serving to produce soldiers and successful men who are rather insensitive to need, as is the case in a patriarchal society). The former terrorist women, on the other hand, viewed the self-awareness arguments as an obstacle to the urgency for action and they 'recycled' the feminist experience (Nadia Mantovani, 1988) into the destruction of anti-abortionist medical practices (Carmen De Stefano, 1988), injuring particularly zealous women jail guards, wanting to count as men at any cost (Silveria Russo, 1990) and, in a more abstract and therefore more dangerous sense, in the radicalisation of choice expressed in armed subversion (Susanna Ronconi, 1988). This is a more dangerous 'recycling' because affection is enlisted to give force to action; it disengages affection from its original 'attachment' and shifts it to a representation (that of feminine oppression) and, thus, allows it to escape realistic examination. That this is probably the case is demonstrated by the absence of feminine self-awareness in the terrorist movement. The female identity of the terrorist was patterned on that of man (Passerini, 1988). Mara Aldrovandi confirmed to us during our meeting that there was no room for discussion on or about women in armed militancy; when there were discussions of communiqués or targets to hit there was no room for personal or mundane problems. And that is not all. Ms Aldrovandi expressed utter contempt for the women who went about smashing the shop windows of Luisa Spagnoli during protest marches because they believed she exploited the slave work of women prisoners:

'It is absurd to create a feminine islet. Communism frees men and women alike' (see Appendices 2 and 3).

North of the Alps, the German psychologist and legal scholar Margarete Fabricius-Band (1978) agrees with this line of reasoning. The author states with regard to the RAF that clandestine life and the relationships formed within the band were devoid of confrontations with one's partner, one's family, one's colleagues at work, one's bosses – the cultural and social movements through which centuries-old female oppression is transmitted. Fabricius-Band also notes that emancipation cannot be abstracted from the concrete situations of life. Women who belong to terrorist groups live in situations in which they are forced to negate economic, cultural and psychological needs. It is somewhat similar to mystical exaltation, but it is also what has been asked of women for centuries, that is, to individually and collectively forego their own needs – and women terrorists accepted this social model totally.

Christina Thuermer-Rohr (1978), the German feminist psychologist, speaks more directly of the significance the large number of women in the RAF had for the women's liberation movement. She says that they constructed an abstract 'people', a 'world proletariat' in whose interests they purported to act and fight: a people utterly alienated, in the grip of consumerism and the power of the media. According to the author they reasoned that since the people had become incapable of recognising their oppression and had lost the will to fight, they forfeited the right to criticise the actions of their 'armed representatives'. But the author also points out that mistrust of thought and action that are purportedly 'representative' of our real interests was specifically responsible for bringing about the women's emancipation movement: women want to act for themselves, they do not want to be represented by anyone else.

While the identity of women in subversive organisations was patterned on that of men, both being combatants for Communism, the data we examined in this chapter indicate a female specificity in the participation in those organisations. We will endeavour to identify it in examining the interviews.

10 THE PSYCHOLOGY OF 'PENITENTISM' AND THE CULTURE OF VIOLENCE

A 1987 Italian law provided for reduced jail sentences for former terrorists who dissociated themselves from armed subversion, recognis-

ing their errors and the tragedies they caused, even though they declined to implicate their comrades. Brunetta (1985) calls it 'dissociation with admission'; Public Prosecutor Armando Spataro (1982)
maintains that with the exception of a few cases it is a dissociation
full of ambiguity, while Luisa Passerini (1988) describes it as dissociation that tracks a social trend. The *Studies on Social Development* of
Brunetta (1985), a study of the two major branches of Italian terrorism, concludes that dissociation with admission found more converts
among members of the Prima Linea, while collaboration with the authorities was more common among the Red Brigades.

At the level of empirical generalisation we can hypothesise that the
culture of violence among the highly-specialised leadership of a strongly
hierarchical armed group leans towards extreme behaviour, such as
absolute non-cooperation or full collaboration, while the culture of
'diffused violence' adapted to the needs of the working class in their
neighbourhoods and factories (Bruno Laronga, see Appendices 9 and
13) fosters 'mediation and compromise between de-solidarisation and
a tenacious desire to erect equestrian monuments' (Silveria Russo, see
Appendix 8).

Bruno Laronga, Silveria Russo and Vincenza Fioroni, all members
of Prima Linea who opted for dissociation, confirm this first empirical generalisation by maintaining that they never fuelled a culture of
suspicion and that they always strived for reconciliation with the penitents, unlike the Red Brigades. This is Bruno Laronga speaking:

> The first point is that we made individual destiny prevail over that
> of the group. Very few thought of their choice in political terms,
> and even fewer were preoccupied with socialising it, even among
> themselves. There is no doubt that if they had waited a few years
> they would have dissociated themselves along with the majority. But
> it was certainly difficult to foresee all this at the time of their ar-
> rest. . . . Moreover, I believe that many of the *pentiti* were more or
> less forced by us to do things they scarcely believed in, such as
> discipline (internal and external). Thus, our major error lay in our
> evaluation of people, all the more so in the case of the more respon-
> sible ones. This means that in Prima Linea, with a few tragic excep-
> tions, the prudent judgement prevailed that one cannot exercise the
> right of making life and death decisions within the organisation. . . .
> It was my lot to have to judge the behaviour of a few comrades
> who were rumoured to be traitors: I never expressed a judgement in
> favour of condemning them to death. . . . Our attitude towards the

pentiti in jail was to try to understand what had happened. They often opted for total scission, in which case they seemed to do nothing but justify their choice, when they did not deny the choice altogether. They carry a heavier weight than we do, and I think they are not at peace with themselves. . . . Finally, we should understand that in many cases it was not the politicians who influenced the municipalities, but the other way around. In the prison world the *pentiti* are considered *infami* (dishonourable), and all the worst things one can think of. Some of them interiorised this concept. (Appendix 13)

When we asked Bruno Laronga why, in his opinion, there were more penitents and hard-core non-collaborators among the former Red Brigades than in Prima Linea (where dissociation prevailed), he answered that this was due to the greater importance given to the collective by Prima Linea than by the Red Brigades.

In fact, social psychology has long been concerned with the importance of the collective in psychological terms. A segregated group structure in which communication between members is reduced to a minimum and where the avenues of communication that may exist pass through the leadership or are under its direct supervision (authoritarian leadership), can have negative effects on the group as whole (see Figure 2.2).

If, on the one hand, there is less opportunity to develop close interpersonal relationships among all the members of the group, thus making the group less cohesive, on the other, the loss of the leader (for whatever reason) can throw the group into chaos. In the case of a leader who functions as a pivotal figure, the 'stellar' structure of the group can go to pieces, since there are no other members capable of operating as 'cohesive forces' (Krech *et al.*, 1984; Swap, 1984).

Things are different in the case of a democratic leadership (as, for example, in the collective Laronga speaks of), that is, a structure that may have as much power as an authoritarian one, but exercises it by stimulating the maximum impact and participation of each member in group activities and in determining objectives. In this case the leader tries to reinforce and foster interpersonal relationship within the group for the purpose of invigorating it and the leader seeks to prevent the development of a hierarchical structure in which privileges and differences in status predominate. As we have seen, where a democratic leadership shows weakness in its relationship to its comrades, perhaps because it is given too much responsibility for political choices, that is where we are likely to see collaborators – at least in Prima Linea.

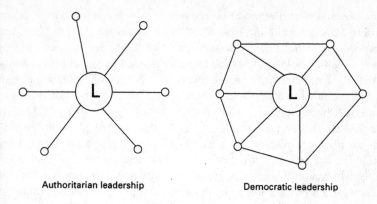

Authoritarian leadership   Democratic leadership

Figure 2.2

As a general rule, when there is greater group cohesiveness, evidenced in collective discussion of problems and in mutual friendships (which are impossible in the regime of rigid compartmentalisation characteristic of the Red Brigades), we are likely to find the following:

1. An effective 'social norm' at work in the group, that is, the development of a 'social norm' that mediates compromises among the various opinions expressed by individual members.

2. A more evident risk-shift phenomenon, that is, a tendency of the group to take decisions that entail a greater risk than individual members would be willing to take alone (Gulotta, 1987). This phenomenon, closely studied in social psychology, presupposes that the strength of the group, its courage and determination, are greater than that of its individual members due to an 'institutional construct' (Krech, Crutchfield and Ballachey, 1962). This 'institutional construct' is a common group faith found among members of almost all established, organised groups, according to which the group transcends the individuals that compose it. It is a belief conditioned mainly by motivational factors; group members tend to identify with the group, but if this identification is to fulfil its function, the referent of the individual's identification must be greater than the individual.

Oddly enough, dissociation can be seen as an example of risk shifting, although at first glance or, rather, from an objective standpoint, it may not seem so. In fact, objectively speaking, the penitents took a greater risk in collaborating, consisting in the danger of retaliation by their comrades still at large; objectively, their choice allowed the democratic State to lower the risk of an authoritarian involution. However, psychology is not just concerned with objectivity *per se*, but with the way in which objectivity is felt and experienced by social protagonists. As with all extreme positions, penitents and obdurate non-collaborationists opt for one of two opposites, namely conformity with the values and rules of the society they had once fought against or all-out animosity to it – 'we still dream with the oppressed masses throughout the world', as an obdurate woman who wishes to remain nameless wrote from jail. The decision to dissociate, in the legal sense, entails a psychological risk that has been recognised as extremely dangerous since the dawn of civilisation: the contemplation of opposites, understanding the contradiction between values which are alternative to Western society's because they are founded on solidarity, concern for the marginalised and the weak, on work as a social service and on obedience to the civil and penal norms of a society that tends to disregard such values. Bruno Laronga stated in answer no. 4 of the questionnaire ('is there anything about your experience in armed struggle that you miss?'):

> the opportunity to face danger together. Relationships not based on interest, our honesty. Today all you see is the interest angle. (See Appendix 9)

The investigative tools supplied by social psychology of groups undoubtedly help to shed light on many aspects of the phenomenon of participation in armed subversion; on the other hand, they leave the fundamental question unresolved: Why is it that women are less inclined to collaborate?

Table 1.1 shows that among the 'orthodox' Red Brigades the ratio of men to women penitents is balanced with respect to the differential participation of men and women in armed subversion; in the 'heterodox' Red Brigades of Lombardy (the Walter Alasia Column), we see a disproportionate number of male penitents. Social psychology answers this question by explaining that the attitude of an individual not only reflects his or her affiliative feelings toward the group, whether they be belonging or reference, but also his or her personality (Krech, Crutchfield and Ballachey, 1962)), which, being unique and irrepeatable, requires investigative tools of a different calibre. And they are, necessarily, those made available by psychological theories based on personality, a field of inquiry in which depth psychology plays a privileged role.

3 Path and Interpretation

1 THE PSYCHOLOGICAL PATH OF THE TERRORIST

> *Reason in my philosophy is only a harmony among irrational impulses.*
>
> George Santayana, *Persons and Places*

The proliferation and intensity of incidents of terrorism in the 1970s and 1980s earned terrorism and terrorists the attention of scholars, government agencies and the mass media. The literature on terrorism has grown dramatically, but there is as yet no agreement on what terrorism is. The Russian revolutionaries (Narodnaya Volya – People's Will) of the late 1870s were the first to develop a theory of terrorism:

> Terroristic activity consists in destroying the most harmful persons in the government, in defending the party against espionage, in punishing the perpetrators of notable cases of violence and arbitrariness on the part of the government and the administration, and it aims to undermine the prestige of the government's power, to demonstrate the possibility of struggle against the government, to arouse in this manner the revolutionary spirit of the people and their confidence in the success of the cause, and finally, to give shape and direction to the forces that are fit and trained to carry on the struggle. (Schmid and de Graaf, 1982)

Terrorism has not changed fundamentally in the hundred years that separate the beginnings of anarchist terrorism from contemporary terrorism. Terrorism does not seek to eliminate individuals by murder; it seeks the collateral effects on persons other than the victim. In this view, terrorism can best be understood as a violent communication strategy: the nature of the terrorist act, its atrocity, its location and the identity of its victim serve to amplify the power of the message. In order for violence to become terroristic it must have witnesses.

The lack of consensus on the definition of terrorism is important because it has an impact on whether or not the perpetrators of an act of violence are labelled 'criminals' or 'terrorists'. One of the most serious attempts to define terrorism has been that of Wilkinson (1974), who defines it as 'the systematic use or threat of violence to secure political ends' and he makes a distinction between four types of terrorism, namely criminal, psychological, warfare and political terrorism. He further distinguishes political terrorism into three broad categories: 'revolutionary', where the systematic use of violence has the ultimate goal of causing radical change in the political order; 'subrevolutionary', where the purpose of terrorist violence is to effect a change in public policy without altering the political order; and 'repressive', where violence is used to suppress or restrain certain individuals or groups from forms of behaviour considered undesirable by the State (Alali and Eke, 1991).

Thus far, the literature suggests that labelling acts of political violence is situationally dependent and idiosyncratic, to wit, it depends on who is being labelled and the party doing the labelling (Chomsky, 1986). Picard and Adams (1991) conducted an interesting study on the characterisation of acts of political violence, commonly referred to as terrorism. The study considered the most frequently used characterisations of acts of political violence and their perpetrators in the *Los Angeles Times*, *The New York Times* and the *Washington Post* for the years 1980–85. The study revealed that a significant difference exists in the way the media, government officials and witnesses characterise acts of political violence and the perpetrators of those acts. The media and witnesses tend to use nouns or verbs that describe what happened, as in 'bombing', 'shooting', 'attack', 'gunman', etc., while government officials tend to use nouns, verbs and adjectives that bear implicit judgements about the acts or perpetrators, as in 'brutal killing', 'despicable action', 'terrorism', etc. Media personnel and witnesses thus tend to use terms that are more objective than those used by government officials.

Much of the literature (Barnhurst, 1991) dwells on the question of why these persons do what they do in an attempt to justify, excuse, condemn, or explain their violence.

The difficulty in devising a non-arbitrary definition of 'terrorist' lies in the fact that there are a variety of reasons that may induce an individual to undertake the path of terrorism. Moreover, diverse reference criteria (legal, criminological, political, social, moral, cultural and so on) influence or determine such definition.

Each definition attempts to explain the phenomenon from its particular perspective. Political scientists have proposed two types of explanations for violent means to political ends. One provides a variety of individual rationales for violence based on the personal perspectives of terrorists themselves. Another proposes that terrorists act because they are otherwise excluded from political life: the state of 'relative deprivation' is what motivates terrorists.

Psychologists suggest that terrorists have deviant personalities (Schmid and Jongman, 1988) and the fear they generate draws force from their involvement in groups. Military scientists consider terrorism a form of surrogate warfare; sociologists have proposed that terrorism is part of the normal level of aggressive behaviour in societies that lack alternative modes of social change (Schmid and de Graaf, 1982; Schmid and Jongman, 1988).

Many scholars, especially in the field of law, place the emphasis on motivational aspects, which, to their reckoning, are the most significant and relevant in the psychological make-up of the terrorist. According to their perspective terrorists fit into one of four main categories (Bassiouni, 1987): (a) common criminals motivated by personal reasons; (b) persons who engage in delinquency due to psychopathological conditions; (c) persons who set out to gain publicity for a grievance or who set out to remedy a wrong; and (d) ideologically motivated individuals who take action for political reasons, real or imagined.

The fourth category (into which the third often merges) lends itself most readily to describe the behaviour of the subversive terrorist, that is, the person who behaves violently in order to defend or promote interests and ideals, and resorts to criminal acts to make a point, either because such a person does not believe it is possible to achieve such ideals by legal means, or because the person perceives partial or outright rejection on the part of the governing political or legal system.

A characteristic of persons who engage in delinquency for ideological reasons is that they consider their actions either dictated by circumstances beyond their control or made necessary by the limitations of the political context in which they operate.

According to Bassiouni (1987), the following characteristics define the psychological profile of the terrorist:

1. heightened perception of oppressive conditions, real or presumed;

2. firm conviction in the possibility of modifying them;

3. realisation that no peaceful efforts to ameliorate conditions are being implemented;

4. belief that it is necessary to resort to violence in order for change to take place;

5. awareness that the likelihood of success is not a pre-condition to

violent action, that it is sufficient for the terrorist act to set the
stage for the desired change;

6. belief that the end justifies the casualties of terrorist action.

A terrorist does not simply weigh risks against the likelihood of
success, as is normally the case, but adds into the equation the abstract value of the cause for which he or she is fighting. This is the
reason why traditional notions of deterrence are ineffective against such
a subject. Unlike a common criminal, he or she does not act on the
basis of a cost–benefit analysis.

In sum, terrorists are able to convince themselves that the end justifies the means, however atrocious they may be, and that the cause
legitimises them and makes a terrorist a hero or a victim, according to
circumstances.

The criteria posited to identify terrorists, which may be very useful
to those who must decide on how to deal with political criminality,
are not very useful in identifying the mechanisms that lead to the assumption of a subversive role. The most obvious shared feature of
those who participated in armed subversive movements was their young
age, as we mentioned earlier. This shared feature suggests that the
psychodynamics of the terrorist choice are rooted in the delicate period
of adolescent development. It is no accident that a 'prescriptive crisis'
is considered typical of youth in adolescent psychology, that is, doubt
concerning authority in general and parental authority in particular in
prescribing conduct and values. This crisis is deeply rooted in the cultural code, that is, the whole system of schemes which through the
generations have proven capable of resolving the problems of members of society itself. The elements of this code constitute the points
of reference of a given culture, its values and its models and they
correspond, roughly speaking, to what in sociology and cultural an-
thropology are termed 'models of behaviour', that is, forms of social
co-existence, traditions, customs, laws and procedures that characterise a given historical moment. Yet, because of its contingent character, this code does not benefit from the strength and stability of the
natural genetic code, which mutates only under the influence of
significant and persistent selective environmental pressures. Unlike the
genetic code, the characteristic models of behaviour and the complex
of beliefs, values and norms that form the substrate of the cultural
code are based on a consensus to transform the arbitrary into the prescriptive, that is, to give force to constructs which in and of them-

selves lack prescriptive character. Man assumes a dual role in the production of this arbitrary code, as carrier and creator of culture and the creation is characterised by discretion, that is, the exercise of freedom within the bounds of the prescribed (Jacques, 1978). The adolescent's task is to acquire a personal identity, to gain possession of the material and cultural means to perform socially useful work, and to learn to channel and dominate aggressive drives. The starting point of the specific psychological path with which we are concerned is the identification of the causes that facilitate adoption of certain types of behaviour by some young people, specifically, violent and subversive behaviour, which are normally proscribed by the cultural code.

We can see from a psychodynamic standpoint that adolescence facilitates transgression against the cultural code. It is an evolutionary period in which a great quantity of libidinous and aggressive drives are set free; a period in which the profound need to love and hate is in desperate search of an object on which to expend its energy.

And there is an absolute need for such an object; indeed, if there is no such object, a monster can be created to replace it. This is borne out in experimental psychology. When Kanisza (1980) seeks to demonstrate the 'weakness' of experience as a factor in structuring the field of perception, compared to the formal factors studied by the Gestalt school, he devises an ingenious experiment consisting in covering first one half and then the other half of a drawing of a horse. Perceptive reconstruction proceeds by amodal completion, as it is called in psychology: one does not see two horses, but perceptively 'constructs' a monster of a horse with an inordinate distance between the two pairs of legs. In other words, the body of the horse under the covered part is completed in an 'amodal' way.

These developmental storms bring into play defence mechanisms against the emerging drives typical of adolescence and youth. As formal thought emerges, that is, the thinking process based on sensible data as well as reversible hypotheses, intellectualisation also becomes available as a means of keeping such drives under control. Thus, by virtue of the mechanism of intellectualisation, the drives are given a name and a meaning within a historical–existential framework as far removed as possible from their original psychological motivation.

With the wisdom of hindsight Mario Ferrandi states:

However the Communist Party bears great responsibility for this, as it taught us to cheat on morality and ethics, inducing us to adopt a double ethical standard, and this leads to a tragic watershed. . . . The first political murder was carried out by Lotta Continua – the Calabresi murder. You must understand that there was a committee against State massacres which even the Red Brigades and people such as Dario Fo and Feltrinelli belonged to. Perhaps Sofri did not actually give the order himself. . . . We found ourselves in the middle of a growing armed struggle in 1976–77 that had a vigilante quality about it.   (see Appendix 5)

While violence by one individual triggers immediate repulsion, the violence of history is understandable and justifiable, at least in hindsight, because it is instrumental in establishing new social orders and liquidating obsolete ones. During adolescent development, intellectualisation gives way progressively to rationalisation, in which intellectualised events and histories are given a metaphysical and causal cogency. An example of rationalisation is F's answer to our request for a second meeting:

No, we have power only over death, not over life – until death supervenes. Then we may love each other so as to delay death as long as possible. But even in regard to this, for me solitude is an ultimate thing, something that the schools of psychology do not take into consideration and there's the rub.   (see Appendix 1)

The choice to live in a cabin in the middle of the countryside, to keep her children from attending kindergarten, is not the history of a particularly intense and felt need for solitude. There is rationalisation at work – that is, giving universal meaning, necessary and eternally valid, to a strategy used by this interviewee to avoid a situation that immediately presented itself as extremely anxiety producing.

Both intellectualisation and rationalisation transform an otherwise unacceptable clash of drives into a way of thinking that can be transmitted and shared (and which is, hence, ego-compatible from a psychodynamic standpoint). Paranoid projection projects destructive life experiences that emerge in adolescence onto some external object by which one then feels persecuted. Opposed to this 'evil' object is a 'good' one in which to invest all the need for affection, sympathy and recognition characteristic of adolescence. Even Silveria Russo suspected she might have engaged in paranoid projection when, in answer to question No. 5 of the questionnaire ('What did your group consider justification for killing an enemy'), she stated:

It was a symbol of oppression, and one that worked well for such oppression. We killed as if we were at war; a war, however, which only we declared. We lived this logic of war in a schizophrenic way, as a series of schisms, a schism between the desire to lead a tranquil life and to belong to a movement, between sentiment and reason. (see Appendix 6)

To bring schizophrenic thinking into play is an obvious rationalisation of the profound motivations that led down the path of armed struggle. But the words of Silveria Russo also illustrate a peculiarity of a successful paranoid projection. When an aggressive drive is placed outside of oneself, an accommodating understanding is reached between the ego, which plans the political murder, and the self-consciousness that judges the ego (the superego). Thus one does not have compassion for one's murdered enemy, but for oneself, because of the impossibility of leading a tranquil life due to the need to fulfil a higher mission. Asceticism simply negates both libidinous as well as destructive drives (Freud, 1967), and the transition to action keeps the ego from interiorising the conflict by unloading it on behaviour that takes place externally.

These mechanisms condition one's behaviour and thought structure at all levels of interaction, from the family microsocial environment, to the social ecosystem, to the cultural macrosystem. Let us examine them briefly beginning with the microsystem. According to psychodynamic theory the process of separation of adolescents from their parents is all the easier the more the set of ambivalent feelings toward parental figures – which psychoanalytic theory terms the Oedipus complex – is overcome in the child's identification with the parent of the same sex and in the transformation of erotic feelings toward the parent of the opposite sex into affection. This is only possible if the intrafamily relationships are sufficiently good, that is, secure and protective; but there must also be a clear distinction of roles and the capacity to respond to the child's aggressivity in such a way as to make it clear that it is possible to 'recycle' deep destructive aggressivity in a way that is useful in adapting to the outside world. A father who is still loved and hated can unleash an extremely powerful need for idealisation in which schizoparanoid defence mechanisms against drives are still at work (by which it is not possible to overcome the Oedipus complex in a positive manner). A 'good' parental figure is idealised (the child idealises a 'good' parental figure) or a particularly loved quality of the father (for example, a strong and confident father, who may actually have been so in reality, but who used his strength too sparingly for the good of the child or at any rate too sparingly from the child's point of view). These dynamics surface in the life stories of many former terrorist women, as in the idealisation of the father, a career military man, in the case of Silveria Russo and Susanna Ronconi.

If the parental figure does not lend itself to idealisation, perhaps because he is good but weak or at least perceived as such, a transitional figure is adopted, someone who is fairly close to the parental figure, as, for example, the Stalinist grandfather in the case of Franceschini (1988).

The life stories and our interviews show that all referents of idealisation were leftist figures, such as old socialists and communists who fought in the resistance, suffered social marginalisation or were forced to emigrate. In cases in which there was a father with lofty ideals who was not strong enough to enact them or whom an unkind fate forced to emigrate (Vincenza Fioroni and Bruno Laronga, see the appendices), the paternal role is reversed, and the child tries to achieve the ego ideal which had been the father's to demonstrate how things should have been done by the father who failed.

The 'failure' of a parent can take on many forms. It can be the failure to give an adequate affective context to the power exercised; the forceful affirmation of ideals; the setting of definite limits and constraints on the aggressive drives and desire for omnipotence of the adolescent; or the failure to provide a stable reference point in the family, something more than occasional appearances, however charismatic (Mara Aldrovandi, see Appendix 3).

What should be stressed is that it is not a question of objective failure; it is a question of how the relationship with the parent was experienced by the son or daughter and this experience is closely related to the adolescent's expectations with respect to the parent. It is a question of what a subject makes of his ideas and feelings and not what the parent was in reality – assuming 'reality itself' is knowable.

Freud (1929) maintained that the primary need of a human being is to love and be loved; thus in order to safeguard love one removes one's resentment for the parental 'failure', and this removal is usually sustained either by a reactive formation (unconditional obedience to the leader) or by external projection of the hostile affection. The result is an idealised parental figure, that is, one that has no shadowy areas, weak points or doubts, because it is based on the removal of these doubts and shadows.

What is plainly lacking in this psychological operation is grieving for the insufficiency of the parental figure; what we find is a process of separation of hostile affection from its origins.

At the level of the ecosystem, what can function as a good support figure for one's projections of bad feelings and representations? According to Fromm (1973), it is anything that threatens man's vital interests – not just physical equilibrium, but psychic equilibrium as well. Bruno Laronga is in accord with this:

> But Bruno Laronga is not the son of the Italy of immigration; I was an aristocrat who worked as a labourer in order to be a militant and I was a militant in order to save the worker from the tyranny to which he was subjected by the company's 'enterprise command'. (see Appendix 19)

From these words we may deduce that the value perceived as most threatened was psychological rather than physical equilibrium, that is, equilibrium characterised by a desire for solidarity with other men, by a framework capable of giving meaning to one's daily actions, by a sense of the effectiveness of those actions, by a subject of devotion.

There are many situations in which the social system can unleash human aggressivity as, for example, when certain social configurations are impervious to change even when it is pursued with the instruments of democracy; when the procedures used by those in power are opaque; when there is a real or presumed disloyalty on the part of the adversary (the policeman who shot Mara Cagol after she had put her hands up, according to Alberto Franceschini); or when there is tolerance for certain forms of criminality. All these instances of social malaise prejudice the legitimate desire to feel part of a movement capable of historically meaningful action, to be devoted to an ideal worth fighting for, and to be able to make a contribution towards bringing about greater social justice.

Yet there are many people who are socially committed and have innovative, even revolutionary, ideas who do not end up being terrorists. The explanation for taking such different paths is to be found in the context of intellectualisation and rationalisation, and in their actual use. When they are used well, they serve to examine reality, that is, they are used in the dynamic assimilation of stimuli that serve as objects for one's cognitive and operative schemes, and therefore for the accommodation of these schemes to factual reality. When they are used wrongly, they lend themselves to a consolidation of schizoparanoid productions. An example of the former is to be found in these words of Mario Ferrandi:

What was most gratifying about armed struggle for me was the pleasure of exercising real power, an effective counter-power against the hypocrisy of the powerful ... but 100 violent episodes on the part of the police against marchers do not constitute a dictatorship ... we should have infiltrated the Carabinieri [State Police] in order to change the State from within and to be humanly better than the people we were fighting against; instead, not only did we fail to do that, but we even failed in affirming a military ethic, and thus we killed disloyally, by stabbing in the back ... (see Appendix 10)

An example of rationalisation as an instrument for consolidating schizoparanoid productions can be seen in the answer of Mara Aldrovandi to the question on the importance of political legitimisation (Appendix 3):

Yes, I confirm that even political murder is acceptable, so long as one does it with the proper degree of awareness. Ethics and politics are one. But politics says that it is first necessary to sensitise the people around you, to wait for a basic legitimisation, and to ascertain that there are no alternatives, and there were no alternatives!

Thus, first a connection is made between one's hostile and aggressive drives and the representation of a collective malaise that could justify them; then one gives the manifestation of hostility an atemporal cogency, definitely separating the representation of collective malaise invested with these aggressive drives from the drives themselves, making political murder a question of conscience.

The separation works all the better if the cultural environment is a macrosystem in which justifiable violence already exists in the form of the violence of an oppressed class against an oppressive, hegemonic class. Whether then the violence allowed in class struggle occurs in the final clash, at the moment of taking power or at another time, is a detail that does not change the legitimation that violence is given in the historical–eschatological perspective. The change that brings about well-being and happiness to the oppressed is, in the end, the fruit of power. A theory of this type necessarily places values such as compassion, respect for life and weakness in a subordinate position and it necessarily restricts others' range of social action, such as solidarity, which is only possible within the group that is 'on the right side'.

In our cultural system, right-wing theories of violence, the myth of the superman and of racial superiority, have not enjoyed much resonance among young people because they lack the totalising character of a Communist Utopia. The culture of right-wing violence (not the massacres, of course, which are for us 'the thing in itself') or, as Fioravanti defines it, 'armed spontaneity', is much closer, from a physiological standpoint, to the relief of internal hydraulic pressure than to a conscious plan charged with powerful subconscious affective forces.

Recapitulating, the emulation of an ideal of a combatant for justice is transmitted directly or indirectly at the level of the microsystem, that is, within the family or one's immediate entourage. This mechanism of pre-constituted socialisation by which one learns directly or indirectly certain sociocultural and political values (a necessary but not sufficient element in the psychological formation of the terrorist) is grafted onto the typical adolescent and post-adolescent urge to acting out. When this deep psychological need to realise oneself through commitment and the impelling need to belong is placed in the cultural framework of a just cause for violence, it can lead to armed militancy, particularly when paranoid projections, also typical of the juvenile phase, meet an ecosystem that offers good support and a group of comrades willing to share the risks and responsibilities assumed by the 'disassociation' of the individual. The concerted pressure from all these factors ends up moulding a personality that sees little or no possibility of assuming a positive identity other than that of a militant to realise political ideals.

These complex mechanisms, largely beyond the control of consciousness, can have a powerful and destructive effect on the freedom and discretionality of thought, to the point of depriving it of its connection to the categories of existence and lead to the pathological degeneration of certain normal thought processes. For example, magistrates, scholars and terrorists themselves have frequently erroneously referred to terrorist thinking as 'symbolic', which is a normal, psychologically healthy feature of thought. But one cannot speak of symbolic thought when journalist Tobagi was killed because he was representative of journalists who had the courage to investigate certain sanctuaries of left-wing culture; on the contrary, thought in this case is bereft of symbolic power and is 'forced' to operate with syncretic ideas of subconscious experience and external referents. As Crespi (1978) points out, such 'symbolic' thought loses its connection with the categories of existence, the 'being-with-others', 'the possibility of risk' and 'pain', which make one's fellow man seem essential to one's own identity. We have a contradiction between what one should be and what one actually is. The latter is deeply rooted in the nature of man, which is a daily existence first and foremost, and an ideal existence in some distant future. Thus, once an idea loses its connection to existence, it becomes domination over others, demanding either total conformity or suppression of differences.

Silveria Russo is perfectly aware of this 'schizophrenia of the idea':

> So I would say that the simultaneous presence of reason and anti-reason was there from the beginning in the desire to create a Utopia (peaceful and communitarian), but also in the belief that only violence is the 'leavening of history' (and this is a precise ideological reference). And, hence, for those who were Catholic, in thinking that the eschatological Utopia could be realised only in symbiosis with other beliefs (in a way, that the Church was rotten in our eyes was just an excuse for giving credence to our option for 'integral poverty,' which was, of course, a political view in any case). And it was right there, in a choice that was of course ideological, that there was the cancer of a split, in the plan as in the persons who implemented it. In the end, I would answer that the split is not between the plan (lucid, noble) and the reality of the men who have to implement it, but between the reality, because it comes first, and the plan. (See Appendix 13)

In Britain, at the turn of the century, the Women's Social and Political Union (the suffragettes) developed a strategy of using violence while providing theoretical justification for such violence.

Official figures show that in the 1970s in Italy terrorism perpetrated by the new Fascists and the left consisted of approximately 14,000 acts of violence, 409 deaths and 1,366 injuries. The Red Brigades terrorist group defined this concentration of violence as a move from a 'creeping civil war' to a 'full-scale civil war' (Bertini, 1978).

According to Kaplan's (1992) interpretation, terrorism directed against the State but strategically carried out against people in Italy shared common underpinnings with a different kind of violence, namely violence against recalcitrant women determined to break the spell of machismo and the value hierarchies expounded in official attitudes of the Church and the State. As Kaplan (1992) concludes, 'the 1970s can only be described as an extraordinary spectacle of open gender-warfare'. The same considerations apply to political extremist and to terrorist activities from the late 1960s through to the first half of the 1980s in West Germany. According to Jacobs (1978), the phenomenon of terrorism was used 'to cast aspersions on and actively suppress criticism of the government form liberals, leftists and feminists'.

A complex of expectations and requirements regulates the everyday life of women, their role in the family, their routine responsibilities and their career expectations. As Gerhard (1993) underlines, the demand for rights equal to those which are taken for granted by men stands in opposition to this allocation of roles. This is because self-determination and equal treatment do not fit in with the care required and the sacrifice expected of the 'family woman'\

2 FEMALE SPECIFICITY

> *When Hercules spins wool at the feet of Omphale, his desire chains him; why was Omphale unable to secure lasting power?*
>
> Simone de Beauvoir, *Le deuxième sexe*

So what is specifically feminine in the evolution of defence mechanisms? The more orthodox Freudian psychoanalytic theory (Freud, 1967; Deutsch, 1977) views the psychological make-up of women as passive and masochistic; these attributes are the 'psychic representatives' of her biophysiological make-up, which predispose women to receive and men to give. Thus, according to this view, males and females are biologically predisposed to assume roles that mirror the specificity of their reproductive functions: to the female's capacity to generate, restricted to the ovulation function, there corresponds the male's capacity for unlimited fertilisation. This basic difference would predispose women to passive–conservative practices and men to dispersive, dissipative behaviour.

Passivity means that the psychological activity of women is rich in introspection and, thus, empathy towards other human beings, while the activity of males is more extroverted and oriented towards the conquest of external space. And it makes little difference whether this is due to the genital trauma, to a girl's disappointment at not having a visible and active organ like a boy or, according to social psychology, to the influence of education and, more important, to her mother's views, according to which 'conquering' is an obstacle to the daughter's adaptation to a staunchly patriarchal society (Ambroset, 1984). Whether anatomy creates passivity, as orthodox Freudians would have it, or a history of restraint, as social psychologists claim, the end result is the same.

Masochism, as it refers to female specificity, means neither moral masochism nor the association of erotic pleasure with suffering, but as the conversion of instinctual energy, especially aggressive instincts, from active to passive, facilitated by women's psychological passivity. Women's greater passivity causes their adolescent identifications to last longer. Thus, boys should identify with their fathers or surrogates and girls should identify with their mothers or surrogates in order to acquire the necessary maternal competency. This path is complicated and may become tortuous by virtue of various interferences. For example, a girl who identifies with a weak mother (who perhaps is not really weak, but is perceived as such, perhaps because she is unable to make people appreciate her merits) in the presence of a strong father who is inattentive to the deeply felt needs of 'his women' (mother and daughter), will have a very different way of relating to others than a girl who has a father who gives her an accurate picture of the world to which she will eventually have to adapt and endeavours to combine the need for ideals with analysis of reality in the right proportions (Winnicott's (1986) 'just enough'). The former will be more inclined than the latter to Manichean divisions of the world into good and evil people, to idealise the former or whoever represents them and despise the latter. In this black-and-white vision of reality, pity, compassion and tolerance of others' weaknesses can be lost. The latter will be more inclined to develop assimilative strategies to absorb the anxiety caused by momentary setbacks without converting it into precipitous action.

It is difficult to identify with a 'weak' mother, whatever meaning this weakness may have or with a mother who shares her daughter's enthusiasms (Giulia Borelli) but is not adequately appreciated by her father (Susanna Ronconi and Nadia Mantovani), even though he may be idealised as strong and self-assured, but is in fact inclined to impose his principles rather than emphatise with the weakness of others (Silveria Russo). There seems to have been a common perception in the psychological path of former terrorist women: a maternal figure perceived as good but weak or, better, strong in her suffering – suffering based on preserving family harmony and integration in the face of the father's affective rigidity or relational shortcomings. These combinations recur often in the life stories of terrorist women and in our interviews with them.

The relationship with this maternal figure may not have been sufficiently protective for the adolescent, although based on affection and tenderness, on a partisan feeling of 'siding with the weakest'. Later on, the young woman shifts these identifications and idealisations outside the family framework, because an examination of reality from within the family is too cogent and presents a reality which is too contradictory with respect to these psychological processes. Thus, a young woman searches for a 'weak person' to love and to save, and a more abstract, removed ego ideal to follow and, by assuming its abstract identity, formulate a plan for its salvation. This ego ideal can very well be an armed group that pursues the annihilation of the strong who oppress the weak. This type of life (and death) solution saves the identification with the weak mother as well, because the young woman assumes her sacrificial attitude towards the family, the husband and the children. The appropriation of the judgement of another, which in our case is the ego ideal of the armed group, is longer-lasting in women than in men because of women's constitutional passivity and masochism.

The love one brings to an ego ideal, idealised in this way, is stronger in women than in men because women tend to sublimate sexual desire much more than men, and thus women also bring this sublimated sexual drive to bear on this love. But the availability of group relationships that attempt to subvert the position of inferiority of women with respect to men, as in the feminist movement, or that interpret belonging to the Catholic religion in a generously radical manner (Margherita Cagol and Silveria Russo), gives a completely new meaning to 'siding with the weakest'. The young woman assumes the sacrificial attitude of the mother as a model, but endows it with universal meaning. Thus, one can sacrifice oneself, but only for an ideal society that is different for everybody, a society which, in the final analysis, is maternal, inasmuch as it is oriented toward need and not profit and emphatises with suffering, but does not impose it as an instrument of growth (see Giulia Borelli's interview; Malagutti, 1987/1988).

If sacrifice it must be, it must involve a commitment on the order of striving to eliminate social injustice in the world, a commitment that must draw from the father's strength in order to be fulfilled, if it is available, or from models outside the family that are radically opposed to the powers that be, such as the partisans in the Italian resistance, the guerrillas in Latin America, the Tupamaros, or the Palestinians. Thus, a woman tends to effect an ideal rather than a real identification. Yet she stands as a model to her own family, assuming the sacrificial role-model of her mother strengthened by the power of the father or of the role-model outside the family. By finding a 'weak entity' to love and save outside the family, a woman demonstrates both to her mother as well as her father what they should have done to use their strength for a 'good' cause, sacrificing themselves constructively.

The terrorist Grazia Grena thought the explanation for her armed subversion lay in the idea of the failed resistance of her father, on the one hand, and in the Internationalism argument on the other – Vietnam, Latin America and so on. Moreover, she and her comrades thought they were proving they were more adept and fundamentally better than their fathers by engaging in armed subversion (Guerra, 1988).

3   THE TWO FACES OF OBDURACY

In your opinion do men embrace armed struggle for the same reasons as women?
  'Exactly', replies Mario. 'But in any case as far as what you are interested in is concerned, I would say offhand that there is no difference between a man's penitence and a woman's, except that women repent viscerally, and hence experience a good many conflicts, whereas for men penitence is an art.'

  'Of course', replies Mara, 'it is an art, just as for a man all life is a continual performance.'

(Mara Aldrovandi and Mario Ferrandi)

The data are unambiguous. For every 100 defendants in armed subversion trials there are only 13 women as against 25 men among the ranks of the penitents. There must be something, therefore, in the dynamic of joining and participating in terrorist movements that predisposes women to greater firmness and obduracy. There must be something extra, not related to the motivational basis common to males and females. Perhaps we should examine first this common basis in order to identify the 'something extra' that motivates women.

Once the 'leap' was made to armed struggle by Italian terrorists, they reportedly operated within the framework of an ideology that minimised individual differences, far more so than is the case for peaceful groups integrated in society. In the case of armed struggle the energy of its adherents had to converge totally against the class enemy, and not be dispersed in compensating for personal tensions. This is how Mara Aldrovandi explains it:

> Human relationships were very gratifying in our common project, but not with regard to communicating personal feelings and doubts. There was no time for private discourse in armed struggle. In this respect we were not well off.   (see Appendix 2)

And Mario Ferrandi:

> In effect, I lived like a hero. Each of us was accepted as we were, good-looking or ugly, and we felt important and influential in re-solving adolescent problems we found ourselves struggling with. And along with these adolescent problems we also resolved social conflicts. We changed names and this was cathartic.   (see Appendix 10)

Changing one's name is cathartic because it allows one to be reborn with a new identity that is played out entirely in the sphere of social conflict. The danger of assuming the identity of a combatant is that one is not concerned with knowing what cards are in play; thus one doesn't know whether the card of adolescent conflict of which Ferrandi speaks has simply disappeared from the deck or is being confused and equated with social conflict. This equation, in the case of Mara Aldrovandi, evidently was not made because she missed not being able to speak about her personal feelings, but she remained in the armed group because the cause was worth the sacrifice.

In substance, the motivational basis common to the two sexes may be the satisfaction of what Fromm (1973) calls 'the desire for unity with other men', which he defines as an existential need, as the ten-sion inherent in being human.

Another common motivational factor for group loyalty and the ideas that this group expresses, may be the fact that armed subversion fur-nishes its adherents with an overriding conceptual framework capable of giving meaning to a whole life, furnishing all the space and time in the world necessary for its realisation. It is very similar to a religious sentiment, and, in fact, this is the way Silveria Russo views it:

> Many of us were in fact Catholics who had distanced ourselves pre-cisely because the Church at that time did not respond to the de-mands of 'integral humanism'. . . . So I would say that the simultaneous presence of reason and anti-reason was there from the beginning in

the desire to create a Utopia (peaceful and communitarian), but also in the belief that only violence is the 'leavening of history'. And hence, for those who were Catholic, in thinking that the eschatological Utopia could be realised only in symbiosis with other beliefs ... (see Appendix 13)

This is an important clarification. According to this interpretation, men found themselves or, rather, believed they found themselves, in the unambiguous situation of protagonists of change. And not just any change, but a change that was held to be of universal import in the long term. Man's desire for effectiveness with respect to the course of social events, found, in a certain sense, realisation in participation in armed militancy.

The 'something extra' of women in this adherence to a strongly homogenising ideology may be the conservation of internal personal tensions and the sense that these should be sacrificed for the greater good of the revolutionary cause. This ideal imposes the general mobilisation of all one's resources in a situation that contemplates, on the one hand, a radiant life in a society made to the measure of man and, on the other, one's own death and that of one's adversary.

What makes this situation so irresistible? According to Vincenza Fioroni it is the following:

The concept and value of being protagonists, in the sense of participating in change, going beyond the concept of delegation.   (see Appendix 12)

Referring to a period prior to her militancy, Susanna Ronconi recounted that there was tremendous energy and cohesiveness in Workers' Power (*Potere Operaio*). They slept very little, stayed up late and worked feverishly at promoting their cause, yet there was no separation between printing flyers and going out to eat together: there was a seamless unity of purpose in their life (Guerra, 1988).

For women to be considered political subjects in an armed group has even greater affective importance precisely because the history of women has been the history of relentless reduction to objects of economic exploitation (with men's connivance) and sexual exploitation.

Vincenza Fioroni states:

The group was very democratic because roles were decided upon on the basis of one's ability, not one's sex.   (see Appendix 12)

In order to understand the violence of women who took part in terrorist movements, as we have seen, we must resort to a variety of explicative models. However, the general frame of reference must necessarily remain related to the specificity of feminine psychology, to the feminine 'way' of living events and situations. We have already seen it: women tend to develop their experience in accordance with an affective model based on sacrifice, on caring for others, on responding to others' needs and on protection. According to this model of life the cause, the meaning of objectives, may be missing entirely or be of secondary importance. When this specific code of living (defined as the maternal–sacrificial affective code) was transferred to the context of armed subversion, it was incarnated in the idea itself of a Communist society or of a just and happy society for all and was pursued primarily by the group as a whole and, secondarily, by the members of the group.

This is Mara Aldrovandi speaking:

> My faith never died. On the contrary! I see Communism as beyond men, beyond the penitents, the dissociated and the obdurate. (see Appendix 2)

What counts is not the performance of the combatant for the revolutionary cause; it is not so much action, which in any event must be submitted to the judgement of others, but one's own experience of the revolutionary ideal, which may also entail dying, not for oneself, but in the name of the group. This is what Silveria Russo means when she states that the schizophrenia, to which she referred in giving her reason why an initial solidaristic drive ended up dispensing death, was really schizophrenia of the group, not hers alone. Her husband, Bruno Laronga, instead, keeps his vigilantism to himself, avoiding dilution of responsibility in the group (see Appendix 7).

The structure of the maternal–sacrificial affective code is the same we see at work in reinforcing intragroup motivation, as Silveria Russo explains:

> With the COLP (Organized Communists for Proletarian Liberation) . . . all the leadership cadres of Prima Linea – most of them men, with a few exceptions like myself, Susanna and Tosi – had been arrested while the majority of women had been able to escape . . . thus they put the group back together in terms of solidarity, even questioning political assassination. The activities of the COLP were principally

robberies for internal financing and for financing the escape of imprisoned comrades. The escape of Susanna Ronconi was organised by them and by the Nuclei of Segio Sergi ... what women gave of themselves to armed struggle was a greater sense of solidarity, a greater ability to stand pain ... (see Appendix 6)

The unconditional and omnipotent quality of this code in relationships with others can also be seen in Adriana Faranda's choice of the cause over her daughter (interview in the daily *Repubblica* of 25 January 1985). Indeed, precisely in order that her acceptance would be total, that society would be transformed into one great maternal uterus capable of completely satisfying the filial needs of men, did Adriana Faranda make the difficult choice of embracing armed struggle in the Red Brigades over her daughter.

This sense of confusion and omnipotence is often associated with personalities patterned on the maternal–sacrificial affective model, especially if this structure is not governed and balanced by what psychologists call the paternal code, that is, the capacity to descend to reality, to recognise and reject contradiction, to give primacy to the moment of performance.

An example of this is this recollection of Silveria Russo:

GB and I wanted to give a feminine connotation to the war. But we were commiserated by our companions ... (see Appendix 6)

In other words, a tragic misunderstanding can be caused by insufficient competency at the level of examining reality, as happened to many terrorist women. They confused the proletariat with the oppressed son to be saved and to be taken up in the grand embrace of the revolution; and they failed to realise that it is not a defenceless creature needing protection, but a mature subject with a long history of developing strategies that are more effective and productive than political murder and knee-capping. The misunderstanding is tragic because it does not lead to embracing children, but to generating monsters.

When, for example, Silveria Russo says that at the time of her armed militancy participation in the firing nuclei was an activity like any other for her, with certain pre-operative feelings similar to those a student might have before an examination, Bruno Laronga exclaims that this was not possible, because it was not an activity like any other; one had to don a war costume in order to be a combatant, as distinct from an ordinary assassin or a war robot.

And this is the heart of the matter, where we must delve more deeply in order to understand the enigma of women's subversive activities. Margarethe Mitscherlich-Nielsen (1978), who was asked to explain the reason for the harshness and tenacity of the women in the RAF, explained that for some terrorist women it may have been a savagely enjoyed triumph to experience a reversal in the dominance relationship between men and women and to see men tremble from their acts of violence; perhaps these terrorist women were showing their mothers that even they could have opposed the domination of the man–father–husband with the same vigour and that, at any rate, they were now sacrificing themselves for the oppressed of the whole world. She goes on to explain that the net separation of feelings of hatred, on the one hand, and idealisation of parents, on the other, makes it difficult for a girl to perceive others as human in their objective psychic reality, to empathise with them, and to tolerate their errors. This incapacity is then abetted by belonging to a group that by way of its negative identification and its restrictive ideative field perceives those who think differently as enemies. Finally, she notes that love of the death game may be seen as a shared trait of all terrorists, but that the women in that game tended to assume in their own eyes and in the eyes of their companions the role of martyrs, precisely because of the sacrificial conduct society has always imposed on women.

The exercise of violence itself set out to have a reparation objective. To the question, 'What justified the killing of an enemy for you?', our interviewees, with the exception of two repentant women, answered that they did not kill lightly. They did it as reparation for injuries suffered, perhaps by others. These were injuries they felt responsible for because they wanted a more democratic society for all, for the friend of a friend whom a despicable psychiatrist had given shock therapy, for women exploited by the anti-abortionist doctor who profited from clandestine abortions, for the detainees of San Vittore jail whom an over-zealous woman guard had tormented, and for the worker whose hands had been severed at the factory because 'somebody' thought it was not necessary to adopt adequate safety measures. Silveria Russo remembers:

Prima Linea was founded in a bar at Sesto San Giovanni by two young men who wanted to become vigilantes, the Robin Hoods. (see Appendix 6)

No doubt the exercise of violence assumed a meaning for Mara

Aldrovandi, who was closer to the Red Brigades than to Workers' Independence, a meaning that was more detached from persons and things:

> Without such violence you obtain nothing; violence has to be answered with violence, there is no other way. At that time there was a good deal of violence, between groups of the extreme left and fascists, between extra-parliamentary groups and the police. I might well have died, as might have died a Fascist or a policeman. In a word, violence was taken for granted and my choice of armed struggle was connected to all that.   (see Appendix 2)

Even though the vigilantism of Prima Linea was viewed by its members as immediate reparation and the mission of the Red Brigades and those close to them was purportedly the elimination of all those who constituted an obstacle to the armed band's ascendancy to power, the significance of reparation was idiosyncratic for the persons who practiced violence; whether such reparation was consummated in the immediate act of violence or in the final result, in the formation of a revolutionary society, the conscious and unconscious legitimisation of it remained unaltered. Even if one killed in a cowardly fashion, by shooting someone in the back, violating the principles of fair combat in military ethics, it made no difference to Vincenza Fioroni, who states:

> The war was just; we designated it a just war ... therefore even political murder was legitimised by it.

Perhaps the history of women's oppression, to wit, seclusion in the family, political exclusion, and exposure to male violence, instituted the dangerous association between active violence and the urge for reparation. According to Susanna Ronconi:

> Feminism will never translate into a 'separate' militancy. However, it will reinforce in a visceral manner the conviction that there is a radical alternative to the reigning social and cultural model. ... It will give full meaning to the term 'liberation', in which subjectivity becomes 'strength' against the paralysing objectivity of marginalisation. (Malagutti, 1987/1988)

The desire for emancipation provides armed struggle with the drive for reparation, ignoring the representations linked to the drive itself. The suffering of a woman who lacks pre-constituted models with which to confront her emancipation does not compel the search for an easy conciliation between private dedication in the family and interest in social participation; rather, it leads to affiliation with a group in which her capacity for self-sacrifice, her willingness to forego her needs in the face of those of her partner, and her ability to conjugate the private and the public are highly prized qualities.

The hostile affection of women, freed of the consciousness of their own suffering, is easily enlisted by a terrorist group that pretends to know what must be changed, that wants to change it here and now, and that on the way to change allows women to manifest precisely those maternal–sacrificial qualities that for centuries constituted recognition of her identity. This combination of the 'something extra' and of the 'equal' can be a particularly attractive feature of armed struggle for women. The 'something extra' as an illusory possibility of change; the 'equal' as the traditional symbolisation of women's role within the group.

In this path leading from adolescent desire to maturation and growth, passing through the affective charging of feminine emancipation and concluding with the assumption of a maternal–sacrificial affective code, emotion and reason are once again joined in women. During the conversation between Mario Farandi and Mara Aldrovandi, the former says that certain women would not have tried Moro only to end up killing him because 'a certain cynicism is specific to men'. Mara answers him that this is due to the fact that women have been expropriated of cynicism.

The hero has always been allowed to be cynical and evil to some extent on the theory that the ethics applicable to common mortals did not apply to him; but no one ever thought the hero's woman should be the beneficiary of such indulgence. Indeed, both the interviews and the statements made at the Vallette Seminar show that men thought of themselves as heros of armed struggle much more than the women did. Bruno Laronga clings to his self-image of combatant. He has contempt for comrades such as V, who did not assume a combatant persona and this quite apart from the fact that V repented; at issue is the 'quality of the combatant', which Laronga thought was deficient, and not the issue of collaboration. Laronga was uneasy with the company of his wife during their exploits (Silveria Russo was not yet his wife at the time of their militancy in Prima Linea, but was his close companion), because her presence added an affective dimension to their operations that jeopardised his 'dignity' (see Appendix 9). Mario Ferrandi admits that a military ethic was never established, but adds that they lived like neighbourhood heroes (see Appendix 10). Of course, there were many variations on this heroic theme. Some militants were mainly oriented toward efficiency of action and therefore loved to surround themselves with 'doers', soldiers who stood by for orders, while others, like Laronga, even tolerated the company of dissolute and inept people, so long as they had a 'war costume'. In the first case we see the traditional military leader, whereas in the second, the partisan leader, who pays attention to the motivation of his companions (see Appendix 13). This experience of being a hero must have been so overwhelming as to be blind to any evidence to the contrary, as Enrico Galmozzi (1990) admits:

> We killed people in front of their houses, in the morning, sometimes even from behind. . . .

On the other hand, true to tradition, women did not live militancy in a heroic way, but in their characteristic manner, that is, 'feeling bad about it, but staying on because it was necessary' (Mara Aldrovandi).

4   WOMEN PENITENTS AND AN EXPLANATION OF THEIR REPENTANCE

What did distancing yourself from the armed struggle mean?
I want to survive and give testimony of my mistakes. The testimony of the dissociating path I have taken is the only message I can send to the relatives of the victims.

Silveria Russo (Appendix 6)

Beyond the various intellectual reasons that can be put forth to explain engaging in terrorism and dissociating oneself from it at a later time, it may be revealing to examine the reasons women penitents themselves gave for their decision.

In explaining her repentance Mara used the defensive strategy of minimising the offence. She collaborated only after being sure she would not jeopardise the freedom of her comrades still at large. This strategy typically includes a declaration of the accidental nature of the event, of the lack of volition and an emphasis on the ideal continuity with life choices made before terrorism, as if to say 'there is nothing new under the sun'. This is Mara speaking:

I repented, if we want to use that term, because in the name of what was I supposed to do 15 years in prison when there was no longer any reason whatsoever for armed struggle, much less for prison? Instead, I got myself arrested. And then it was by chance that I did not opt for total non-collaboration, because I did not end up in Palmi where my world would have been limited to just my obdurate comrades and only with them would I have felt and desired, as Betti Pasqua Aurora says. Don't underestimate prison and the effect it has on people.   (see Appendix 3)

In the course of her interrogation by Judge Armando Spataro (8 May 1980), F resorts to the same strategies to explain her participation in Prima Linea:

I thought Laura (*nom de guerre* of Silveria Russo) and her boy-friend's stay at my house would last only a few days. Instead it went on and on and I had to go out to do the shopping every day. I asked them to find themselves another place to stay, but then I ended up renting them a house at Sanremo. . . . Once the rental period at the house in Sanremo ended, Laura and Andrea (*nom de guerre* of Bruno Laronga) wanted to return to my house. I didn't want this. At the same time, however, I was persuaded to rent a house for the summer . . . during our stay at the villa at Castiglione we checked around for a bank to 'do'.

The subtext here is that they acted extemporaneously, without voli-tion or intention; recurring phrases like 'ended by' and 'however, I was persuaded' in F's oral interrogation seem intended to avoid a clear nexus between action and criminal design. Repentance, on the other hand, recaptures volition and design:

I was confident we could grow, that we could change. We wanted to change society, but we were not changing ourselves and the measure of change is oneself . . .   (see Appendix 1)

Even F tries to emphasise continuity with what went on before, and the essence of this continuity was supposedly the desire for change, to the effect that 'first we wanted to change, but we did not change, and now we are indeed changing'.

Mara Aldrovandi tried to minimise guilt for repentance, and F tried to minimise guilt for belonging to Prima Linea.

The case of F is emblematic of a transitional phase between common criminality and political criminality. F lived her weakness as strength, identifying with the strength of the group. True, she did not know how to shoot, but she did know how to take care of the wounded. She was indispensable in providing them with first aid. However, she refused to visit the dead on-site, because she feared she would think less of the group if she were confronted with the reality of murder. The affection that was given her in exchange for her assistance was very gratifying to her, and it was enough for her; it was even able to compensate for the savageness she saw in her 'armed' women companions (see Appendix 1). Once gratification for returned affection ended, once the leaders who gave her strength and ruthlessness by identification were imprisoned, F had the good fortune of being assigned to a judge, a man who was on the side of those she once despised by proxy, who gave her some time and space limitations in which to take decisions. He told her 'There is prison, but then again there is the possibility of returning to freedom. If you entrust yourself to the State, I will stand as guarantor for the State; there will be a law on repentance, and then I will help you as best I can.' With these words the judge who interrogated F elicited in her that same feeling of security, protection and acceptance of feelings and thoughts (jail might have driven her out of her mind) that was at first the function of the armed band and, thus, names were named with the same ease with which the bicycles used in the assassination of Judge Galli were repainted. Once again the mechanism of identification with the strongest was triggered. But what are the conditions that favoured this? One possible explanation may come from a psychological analysis. F in all likelihood experienced an armed struggle according to a filial code, that is, asking for gratification and affection and activating just enough of the identification mechanism to make her feel strong, secure and protected.

We should immediately clarify that we can see male behaviour in this psychological framework as well. From the statements of Silveria Russo and Vincenza Fioroni it would appear that this was the way in which penitent V experienced armed struggle (shooting was gratifying to him). The interview given to Zavoli in 1990, on 'the Night of the Republic' by Patrizio Peci, leads us to suppose that even the great penitent of the Red Brigades functioned according to this type of code – the man who remembers above all of General Dalla Chiesa that he had given him the impression of a man who did not want to deceive him and who already knew many things about the Red Brigades.

Silveria Russo's reasons for dissociation were different. She did not meet a judge who gave her the impression of knowing how to be strong without abusing his strength; she realised instead that the images of death did not portend an idea in the future, but only what was evident on its face, that is, death. Casting about in a sea of contradictions, Bruno Laronga says that there is a magistrature that abuses justice, there is capitalism that deprives workers of any ideal class reference in exchange for congruous salary increases, and that he misses the gang terribly (see Appendix 9), but that killing is wrong. There remains obduracy as a flexible strategy of dynamic assimilation of the reality of one's own cognitive and operative schemes and of accommodation of these schemes to reality itself. We believe it is no accident that this strategy of penitentism was adopted by a woman (Mara Aldrovandi).

5 POLITICAL CRIMINALITY AND OBDURACY: A PROGNOSIS

Sweet revolution, I wish my woman's tears could turn into bullets.

Graffito at a school in Milan

If we wanted to use the leads this inquiry has furnished concerning the motives for women's greater resistance to repentance for prognostic purposes, we would have to say that the affective codes proved to be the most useful psychological interpretative tool. In essence, a militant who participates in armed subversion according to a filial affective code (that is, asking for gratification and affection and identifying by just the amount necessary to engender a sense of strength and security) is more likely to repent than a militant who fights according to a paternal type of affective code (de Cataldo Neuburger, 1992).

Judges have considerable experience with criminals following a filial affective code. They tend to be gregarious and fanatically tied to their leader, of whom they demand little in the way of understanding, but a lot of action. This does not mean that repentance is a foregone conclusion; it only means that under the right circumstances this subject is likely to collaborate with the justice authorities. What triggers this subject's collaboration is seeing strength coupled with the perception of the good use of that strength, because a subject following a filial affective code identifies with the person who realises this strength. In essence, an individual with this psychological conformation should be furnished with a potent substitute for the prior identification. Women are more likely to repent than men if this type of affective mechanism is operative. Indeed, women have a greater capacity for identification, a greater capacity to internalise aggressivity from the external world (female masochism), which allows them to support more easily than men a sadistic, involuntary streak in the exercise of strength.

It should not be surprising that in the framework of the filial affective code repentance is more likely in political criminality than in common criminality, because in the former the 'filial gluttony' has fewer opportunities for satisfaction. The killers of Prima Linea were 'paid' only psychologically, while those of the Mafia, for example, receive money or job security for each dead body.

The paternal affective code, on the other hand, stands in the way of repentance. We have seen the way this psychological scheme structures personal experience and renders it more stable with respect to change. Specifically, the principle of performance applied to one's own behaviour makes the militant live like a hero; he deludes himself that political murder can be compatible with the dignity of a combatant. As we pointed out in the case of the maternal–sacrificial experiences of women who fought in armed subversive movements, even here we find alienation from the place in which this code could have been used properly and a lack of other suitable external places. These anomalies ensure that these codes, both the maternal and the paternal, will function without limits, without constraints. For example, the hero who demands the best performance of himself in the defence of the weak and the oppressed, that is, work that is oriented towards need and not towards individual utility to the point of the utmost sacrifice, is unconcerned with the needs of the persons his action leaves grieving.

It is easy to see that in this situation it is much more difficult to predict and create conditions that facilitate repentance. From the data collected we may conclude that in these cases penitentism is more likely to occur under casual, at times tragic, conditions than in controlled situations. The path of critical revision begins for some of our interviewees even before disassociation and, hence, arrest, because the soldier's code of honour has been irreparably, albeit involuntarily, broken by producing a fungible victim where the victim of armed struggle may have been a unique, irreplaceable victim. These are circumstances, however, that occur often in war, precisely because violence is a game in which one loses oneself, as one of our interviewees noted. If the hero is made aware that he too has skeletons in his closet, just as he is wont to point out about the people he hates, the illusion of sacrifice as a screen for one's own personal aggressivity should fall apart.

The least encouraging prognosis is reserved for the militant, man or woman, who lives armed struggle with a maternal affective code. That is, a terrorist who identifies with the ideal mother, who is generous, fundamentally good and unlimited in her resources, capable of giving pleasure to her children, and who contains everything within herself in an undifferentiated state.

Such a militant may even be capable of accepting the hatred of the child that betrays, but cannot resist his demand for love, that is, for loyalty to the cause. An affective make-up of this type disperses blame right from the beginning in the identification of ideological truth with the son, so that what becomes responsible for so many tragedies is the ideology itself, and not one's own investment in the ideology. A mother who gives everything to her child has nothing left for herself, not even blame.

Terrorist women bring criminal activity to their investment in the drive for life without need for objective confirmation, because a mother does not owe any performance: it is sufficient for her simply to be.

A maternal disposition controlled by a paternal code implies, on the other hand, that the mother is not good in and of herself, but only in so far as she is a mixture, in the 'just enough' amount, of availability and frustration in order that the child may grow up knowing there are limitations on the demands he can make on others and will not inflict too many frustrations on others. It is much easier to find a woman who lives with an affective code of this type because women have always been asked to live according to this code. Indeed, this code is inscribed in women's broader biological code, which prescribes that women's parental investment in her children will be far greater than that prescribed for men (Barash, 1980). It is easier to find women who function with the maternal–sacrificial affective code in political criminality than in common criminality because, as was mentioned, the ego ideal of the group oriented towards the future is far less sensitive to objective confirmation than the ego ideal of the Mafia don or the leader of a band, who must guarantee protection here and now. The sacrificial experiences are all the more potent in their derealising effect the more they are part of an overall design for the salvation of everybody, in which even the dead acquire the dignity they lacked in life.

The illusion of the great mother of political criminality is that she even claims the victims of her actions as her children.

6 CONCLUSIONS

> *No one who understands the feminist movement, or who know*
> *the soul of a real woman would make the mistake of supposin*
> *that the modern woman is fighting because she wants to be a*
> *man. That idea is the invention of masculine intelligence. Woma*
> *is fighting today, as she has all the way up through the ages*
> *for the freedom to be a woman.*

> Anne B. Hamman, 'Professor Beyer and the Woman Question

The object of an inquiry is not merely to find answers that can be shared and are intellectually productive with regard to existing problems, or to understand more fully what common sense tells us, but to raise issues that keep our thoughts from becoming fossilised. Sigmund Freud said that the sleep of reason generates monsters. We might say that the immobility of reason produces death, since an idea abstracted from the confines of existence of which it is a part as a window on meaning ('the only life worth living is one that satisfies need and no profit'), frozen in a timeless ideal, does not comprehend weaknesses and contradictions and does not allow for effective compassion (because the compassion of 'I am sorry I killed him, but it was a tragic necessity', is a psychological alibi and not effective compassion for the victim) and, in the end, needs death to maintain its purity and its identity

In researching the psychological path of the terrorist, we dwelled at length and in depth on the psychodynamic mechanism that underlie the phenomenology of idealisation and on the reasons that might explain the greater resistance of women to repentance. These are reasons as we have seen, that are rooted in the specific feminine experience in the alienation of the maternal–sacrificial code by which women lived armed subversion. Within that living experience blame is easily dispersed at a level preceding mentation in which internal experiences of frustration, paranoid projections and homicidal drives coalesce. From this coalescence (which in technical language is called symbolic equation) the 'genital' category of understanding is excluded, that is, the keeping to oneself of the pain of contradiction between what one would like to do for the oppressed with an eye towards history and what can actually be done with respect to others' lives. The sense of one's own greatness and importance that characterises the male experience of the hero is limited by the soldier's honour code, on which the dignity of the combatant depends. This specific point of reference makes it difficult to exempt one's own behaviour from an objective judgement which would clearly indicate that to shoot someone in the back is not very heroic. Men, therefore, are more open to repentance than women (and this is the finding that may have prospective utility in the justice system), because it is certainly easier to substitute illusory limits with real limits – easier than creating limits *ex novo* to induce militants who lived by a maternal–sacrificial code to repentance. This is the main reason why the figure of penitent as 'successful moralist' finds much less support among women than men. Penitent women who lived armed struggle by the maternal–sacrificial affective code remain 'manqué moralists'.

These succinct, isolated psychological notations give the measure of the great grey areas surrounding the feminine experience and the ambiguities that derive from it. Women seem destined to be present in all the episodes of subversion, yet ever excluded from the results. When sacrifice, giving of oneself, courage, abnegation – in sum, the entire feminine capital – are transposed from their natural environment, they reveal themselves to be a bankrupting investment, because they are unable to affect reality.

When women give in to the desire to trash convention by the sensational rejection of a role they never chose for themselves, but was assigned to them by those who wrote their history, they are destined to suffer a tremendous loss of identity. They find themselves in a place that does not recognise their differences and problems, and they discover that they no longer understand themselves or other women ('women in armed struggle do not understand women, they are estranged from being women, through militancy . . . they can become perfectly autonomous, but they do it by radically negating themselves' – Franceschini, 1988).

Brigit Daiber recounts that the relationship between women in subversive organisations was so conditioned by the domination of men that they were not able to have spontaneous relationships amongst themselves or to organise against the men (Fare, 1979).

As one of the women of Subversive Aktion of Munich testified, many women chose to join militant groups and there they fell silent. What reduced them to silence was mainly repression by the State, but they also fell silent because they had to hide their history and their perspective behind armed action and the controlled language of the bands.

The tension caused by the struggle 'outside' leaves no room for internal tension. One of the woman terrorists explained that all individuality in armed bands disappears; one becomes the struggle, the objective, the function and the signal. What counts in such male-dominated groups is group cohesion, and the problems of women are small potatoes.

One woman, a former member of the NAP, commented that men organise reality in rational schemes, they decide on the strategy of the struggle on the basis of abstract, but precise, political considerations. Women, on the other hand, are oriented towards practical life and, the other side of the coin, to fantastic production. They are used to small, concrete daily acts that modify reality in a visible and immediate way. And it is in this ant-like concreteness that their imagination, their fantastic dimension, is rooted. Men, this woman went on to say, arrive at fanaticism under the yoke of their ideological schemes, while women, most of the time, are driven by the violence of their dreams. And, with regard to the delay in the birth of feminist protests, this woman stated that the motive was the passivity of women, their 'interior jail', the need for chains, the desire for expiation, because sacrifice is rooted in their being. This need to give without reserve, but also to pay, to overpay in an almost religious way – this woman went on to say – is not a sickness; it is a way of legitimising themselves in some way, as if only through expiation is it possible for them to conquer the right to be armed, to be esteemed, to be considered – in other words, to achieve a sort of reflected identity.

Here, in armed subversion, we find that the risk of an extreme search for supplementarity between men and women is laid out in an extreme manner. When the qualitative difference, which is essential because it renders the two sexes complementary, reaches extreme levels, it ends up erasing every difference and, thus, all tension towards the other. Women in armed struggle become totally interchangeable with their comrades in arms, physically and psychologically; the *mulier* becomes the *vira* of archaic Latin; women correspond in all and for all purposes to men; they are exact duplications. Even the great feminine figures of Ariosto and Tasso fight with men in a climate of equality, but here the lack of symmetry that generates erotic tension is always ready to emerge. At a certain point 'the woman warrior stops, takes off her helmet, shakes loose a cascade of hair, and the truth is revealed' (Mathieu, 1972). Here the symmetry of the armed woman who injures and attacks is nothing but an artifice aimed at developing the greatest tension imaginable. It is thus that women assert their equality

In the context of subversion, women instead seem forced to depolarise their femininity, to transform themselves into androgynous beings ('Mara Cagol', says a friend who shared a period of political militancy with her, 'looked like a boy, good-looking, with a small face and short hair').

In the revolutionary world women replicate men exactly, in all their functions, to the point of losing or renouncing even their own function as mothers. This equality empties the relationship of all tension. 'The woman warrior of Ariosto in her shining armor, sword in hand, is the pole of attraction of a difficult femininity; the woman worker in overalls, with a wrench in her hand, is not that at all. Her assumption of male clothing and position not only fails to accentuate sexual polarity, it tends to neutralise it. The symmetry with the male, playful there, is terribly drab here' (Mathieu, 1972).

Women end up with experimenting a total estrangement from their position, an indifference that borders on lack of respect for their reasons and their thoughts given the impossibility of confrontation and real dialogue.

At this point a woman may even decide to assume her nocturnal *persona* again.

On 30 July 1977, two women commissioned to murder the banker Juergen Ponto (one of whom was his adopted daughter) knocked on the door and offered Ponto a bunch of roses; then they shot him. According to Hilse Korte-Pucklitsch (1978), the significance of the existence of a woman consists in transmitting and protecting life. If this typically feminine meaning of life does not find any possibility of realisation, if the future appears without prospects, without hope for life, the vital energies of women can be transformed into energies of death: one who does not live life must die. The detail of the roses, Korte-Pucklitsch explains, can also be viewed as a symbolic gesture: roses are given to women as a gift and as a way to deny them, at the same time, a life of their own and the right to introduce themselves as a feminine element into society.

Nadia Mantovani observes: 'Today I ask myself how much this rupture [with the bourgeois way of living] was not an exclusively masculine reality, thought and concrete possibility. The profound needs of women remained living as a couple and love. Where did our need to be loved coupled with a habit of fidelity end up? It was a leap in the dark' (Guerra, 1988).

And so it was.

If women lose themselves so easily, it is because they do not know themselves. Women have never told their story. Their story has been told for them by men, and this story has fixed their faces in a social mask that has ended up definitely covering their very lineaments. To take the mask off now is a very risky proposition. Nobody can say what lies beneath it. The mask is the only *persona* in which women in some way are still able to recognise themselves. It is a lie that has become true by sheer repetition.

No doubt the adventure of armed subversion was for women yet further tragic proof of their ephemeral social dimension. But at least they began to tell their story in the first person. They began to re-coup, along with what had always been granted them by 'right' – knowing how to suffer and to pay (and the resistance to penitentism is perhaps further proof of this) – even the right to tell their own story.

The first warrior to fall on the battlefield of armed subversion in Italy was a woman, Mara Cagol.

4 Meetings and Questionnaires

Appendix 1: Meeting with F, 4 March 1990

She was the first penitent of Prima Linea. Arrested in May 1980 as a co-defendant of Sandalo, she was sentenced to three life terms as an active participant in three murders, including those of Judge Galli and the ICMESA Company engineer Paoletti.

However, with the reductions in sentence and the incentives of law no. 354/1975 (which provides under article 54 for a deduction of 45 days for each separate 6-month-period of sentence served by prisoners who have shown a willingness to participate in the work of rehabilitation), F did a total of four and a half years in prison.

In prison she met her future husband, 7 years younger than herself, the penitent V, who was also from Prima Linea.

F is now 35 years old and has three children who were born in quick succession as soon as she left prison: M, the oldest, who is 5 years, R three and a half-years; and V, 7 months. She lives in the province of Mantua in a farmhouse surrounded by fields, which was chosen especially for the children in order that they might have all the room they need for play.

Neither M, nor R, nor V attend pre-school because, according to their mother, the local nursery school follows the regressive practice of separating the boys from the girls.

What was the occasion of your joining the armed conflict?

When I was contacted by members of Prima Linea (1977), and not just by any two members but by the two founders, I was a labour consultant, that is, 'I was working for the owners' and I had a divorce (1976) behind me and was leading a fairly comfortable life. I suffered real poverty later, after I left prison.

What role did you have in the armed band?

I had the logistical support function: I kept chiefs of the national command like Susanna and members of the 'firing squads' like 'Laura' and 'Andrea' in my house. The first militant they brought home to me had been wounded and I liked to care for the wounded, but I did not like to go to see the dead. When they asked me to do that, to go identify someone after a shooting, I did not go. I was in favour of the killings, but I was afraid that when I saw those who were killed, the group would go down in my opinion. I preferred that my connection with them be that of an underling.

What was your chief reason for joining the armed struggle?

The pervasive feeling of the youth being powerless to change things and an impatience with waiting for the birth of a more just, freer society. But then our relationships were not free, the very fact of our freedom being limited, which was true both for 'those who were out of jail and those who were undercover', had the effect of hardening our minds.

How did you think of yourselves in relation to the 'cause', as direct artificers or as its instruments?

I did not think of myself as anything at all. But nobody was free anyway, not even the head. It was impossible to do otherwise once the decision had been made. We wanted to create a more just society, but we ourselves did not become more just, we did not mature, we did not progress and the yardstick of progress is oneself: we never talked about intimate things, personal things and that would have been a good thing to do. The women lost their true character, they were just women combatants; it was the men predominantly who ran things and affections had to be tenuous because one of the partners might unexpectedly wind up in hiding. Stability in affections was a privilege few had.

What was there about joining Prima Linea that most gratified you?

My comrades had only an instrumental relationship with me: I was useful to them and I was glad that I was useful to them, that I was indispensable to them. That was really it, the fact that I was indispensable to them.

Did the idea of considering yourself great and important play a part?

I tried in any case to keep away from any feeling of my being important as a woman of Prima Linea; I considered it something dirty.

Precisely because human relationships were very important to me, when I was arrested and met the police, they were no longer enemies to be struck down but persons. Everything considered, they did me a favour in arresting me.

It would seem that the restrictions of imprisonment helped you to give shape and form to what had previously been confused. . . .

Yes, I liked the physical restrictions. They were good for me. Prison did not hurt me at all. But my husband had a very bad time. Everything considered, he was my first child. At that time I was already leaving the organisation and it was a leap in the dark since I did not have the kind of fiancé who might have made the leap easier.

I suffered a good deal of anguish when I betrayed my comrades, but as time goes on I think that there was no need to suffer so much anguish.

But I wanted to change and I felt sure that this was possible. And then I came back here where I grew up and everybody knows me.

Did the armed struggle leave only pain behind or the possibility of a cultural legacy as well?

Anger, just a lot of anger, like the desire for revenge of the relatives of the victims . . . because I feel panic when I remember their eyes when they demanded that I be made to suffer, and anyway nothing can be changed. And anger inside me for ending up in the armed struggle because the rules for getting along in society had not been explained to me.

I do not feel guilty, you see, no more responsible than that engineer of ICMESA, no worse than those who, when we killed the ICMESA engineer, thought as they sat in front of the television that we had done well, and how because of the fact that I have three murders behind me, I do not feel guiltier that those who deafen my husband in the factory by causing a constant loss in his hearing; not more violent than those policemen who recently maltreated students in the universities.

Aggressive drives are a part of man, I can assure you of that.

Violence is indeed part of man, but one can keep it under control only if one has a good reason for doing so, and the only valid reason is loving oneself. Loving oneself, and thus controlling one's own aggressive drives, means respecting the essence of man as a social animal. . . .

As far as the trial goes, I think they railed at me only because of their pain inside (the lawyer for the complainants called me a whore). That is fair, but not decent.

I take it that for you justice was something above men.

The individual men who administer justice may very well be very capable, possibly even good. But there are also some who treat you worse than a dog. The fact is that we have power only over death and not over life until death comes; so the system of justice too can only administer death.

You are now living with a good deal of life around you; today your parents came to visit you and your husband has a job, and perhaps by using suitable means he can change working conditions without killing engineers and foremen....

No, we have power only over death, power I say, and then we may love each other so as to delay death as long as possible. But even in regard to this, for me solitude is an ultimate thing, something that the schools of psychology do not take into consideration, and that is where things fall apart.... Solitude is something I care a good deal about now, but I give all of you my best wishes for success in your work.

Appendix 2: Mara Aldrovandi, 7 March 1990 – Questionnaire

1.
What were the family relationships in your original family? Do you have a favourable recollection of your family?

Yes, my parents never made me go without anything. That does not mean that they were rich or that they gave me things that were not necessary, but that with them I had a secure loving relationship.

Have you ever idealised one of your parents or a substitute for one of them?

No. My father was the only male figure. He was a typical head of family who knew how to resolve difficult situations and whenever he had time stayed with us and gave us time and attention. My father let me travel a good deal. My mother was the classical attentive mother who managed the family with tenderness and strength. We had some very nice times. They always helped me a lot, both when I was in hiding and when I ended up in prison.

Did you ever have the feeling that you were deprived of something vital, something very important, in your childhood, that you were lacking something which it was your right to have?

No, I always had everything I needed.

I would like to know how you felt about belonging to the armed struggle with regard to family dynamics. In opposition? (For example, the family did not want to discuss social problems and the class struggle.)

I did not flee from my family. Rather, I had to exclude it from my political choice because that was part of the regime governing all militants in the Red Brigades. I still think that that kind of behaviour was right because one could not endanger one's family members or use them for one's own ends.

As a continuation? (The armed struggle manifests at society level what has already been experienced in a conflictual family situation.)

That is not my case at all.

As an escape? (Better the armed struggle than the family.)

No, that does not apply to me either.

2.
Tell me about your reasons for joining Prima Linea. It is not really the political analysis that interests me, unless you want to go over it. I am curious above all to know what feelings led you to join the armed struggle: love of the cause?

I do not like that definition. I was in love with class warfare, which then spilled over into armed struggle.

Dedication to a cause out of deep conviction as to its rightness?

There were people dear to me who stopped short of involvement in armed struggle, the man I loved, for example. My sister was in Avanguardia Operaia (Workers Avant-garde) with me but did not make the jump to armed struggle. But I went in search of something that would give value to the lives of everyone, not just mine I mean. More than dedication to the armed struggle, I am convinced there was no other alternative.

A sense of your own greatness and/or of your own importance?

No, but I discovered that many people took that path for reasons of that kind.

3.
What was the occasion of your joining the armed struggle?

(a) Group friendships?

I was a militant in Avanguardia Operaia and then I was introduced to Reparti d'Attacco (Attack Detachments), which, however, broke up in a short time. Finally, I went into the Red Brigades.

(b) I was selected because I was already a sympathiser?

Yes, because if I were not already a militant in an armed group they would not have accepted me into the Red Brigades like that, from one day to the next.

(c) I still do not understand what brought it about?

No.

4.
What justified the killing of an enemy for you?

(a) It was necessary for the cause but I felt badly about it.

One was killing one's opponent, the class enemy. And we did not like it for the man who died or for his family members who wept over him. But in any case when you get into class warfare you either become an independent terrorist in the Palestinian manner or you go into a movement. I liked very much the writings of Che Guevara who recounted the pain he suffered when he had to kill. I have met men who have killed many times (AM), but I assure you they were very tender hearted.

(b) He was an oppressor or a symbol of oppression or one who worked zealously for those in power.

I have never been an enthusiast about justice like 'the father of my son'. For me, enthusiasm about justice is moralism. The important thing is that without violence you do not accomplish anything. However, Mara Cagol tried to do things differently before founding the Red Brigades. I, too, before going as far as armed struggle put in years and used different means before.

(c) Nothing justified the killing of an enemy.

5.
What, above all, did the armed struggle mean for you?

(a) Annihilation of the oppressors?

(b) Creation of a more just society?

We did not think we would see a Communist society at the end of our struggle, but we believed that our commitment would help create it. When you have faith you can keep going even without concrete results. In any case we got results in the factories and in the working districts.

6.
If the armed struggle was supposed to create a world based on justice, did you consider yourselves the direct artificers or the instruments of this creation?
   Did you ever have a feeling that you could not have done otherwise?

It was the only thing possible. As I told you, we would have gone on even without positive results because we had faith. In effect we were only the instruments of this creation: we did not believe we would see it at the end of our struggle.

7.
Were there moments when you had doubts about the armed struggle or were you always in a symbiotic relationship with it?

The divisions within the Red Brigades, seeing the upsetting effect of power in the group, were all things that disappointed me and made me think and then keep my distance, at least psychologically.

8.
What was there about your militancy that most gratified you?

(a) A sense of defiance of society?

No.

(b) Human relationships in the group?

The human relationships were very gratifying in the common project but not in the personal communication of feelings and doubts. There was no time for private conversations in the armed struggle. From this point of view we were not in good shape.

(c) Interchangeability of roles: both women and men can shoot and kill, both women and men can be heads of logistical and operational networks.

Yes, Mambro is right when she says that women have won a position of equality in the armed struggle.

9.
**Have you ever felt tension between your femininity and
belonging to an armed group? Did the experience you had
enrich you or did you feel that you had to give up a part of
yourself? Having listened to interviews with women who were
formerly terrorists on 'La notte della repubblica' (the Night of
the Republic), I got the impression there was a kind of
hardening in your women comrades. Can you confirm or deny
this impression?**

No, I deny that. We were all soldiers. It is just that at that point you
do not put on a big show because you do not want to make the sweat-
shop work of the women prisoners profit Luisa Spagnoli. It is a question of responsibility. Or rather, even more. Feminism is in conflict
with Communism. We cannot make a women's island within the Communist revolution, which, by definition, liberates men and women.

10.
What did distancing yourself from the armed struggle mean?

(a) Could you describe it as an emotional feeling?

No, choosing armed struggle was an emotional feeling.

(b) Moral uneasiness?

Disgust with comrades influenced by personal motivations.

(c) Desperation?

[*Unanswered.*]

11.
Why the cooperation with the justice system?

[*Unanswered.*]

12.
**If you had to describe your former comrades' naming you as an
accomplice, what would you call it?**

A person who puts the safety of others at risk is a bad person, but I can understand a woman comrade of the Red Brigades involved in the Dozier kidnapping, who, after having been kept in prison for 15 days with a bullet in her leg, said: 'Forgive me, comrades, but I cannot stand it any longer!' I never heard a man say anything like that.

13.
How did you feel about the police who caught you and the judges who tried you?

I met a magistrate who was very humane with me, very personal in his relationship. He helped me a good deal later.

14.
Did armed struggle leave behind any possibility of a cultural legacy or just a great deal of pain?

The lived history of a generation to think about. The values of this generation that are still asking to be realised.

15.
What things do you now consider important in your life?

Values. Those are what I always think are most important in life.

16.
Is there anything in your life that you would like me to ask you about? Any questions of the interviewee for the interviewer?

How is it you did not end up in the armed struggle?

Appendix 3: Meeting with Mara Aldrovandi, 7 March 1990

Mara A. had never before granted interviews.
  She was watching 'Notte della Repubblica' [the Night of the Republic] when I arrived at her house in the suburbs of Milan at 9:30 p.m.

We began to talk after saying goodnight to her child, who had waited up for me.

On 'Notte della Repubblica' they were showing the interview with Mario Ferrandi, whom Mara calls 'the father of my son'. By the way, she is a psychologist like myself.

She began the conversation.

She told me right away that I would not be able to understand Mara Aldrovandi, the terrorist of Reparti Comunisti d'Attacco (Communist Attack Detachments), without knowing her background.

'I worked in Avanguardia Operaia (AO) [Workers' Avant-garde], which then merged with Democrazia Proletaria [Proletarian Democracy]. I think that many chose armed struggle for psychological reasons. At that point I left, because DP was too inclusive for me. I went into armed struggle through a rational decision based on a sentimental feeling. However, I think that many chose armed struggle for psychological reasons, possibly referring to family conflicts not resolved in a mature way, but in any case reasons that had nothing to do with class warfare.

I did not fall in love with a man and follow him into the armed struggle: the man I loved before, when I was still in AO, stopped short of embracing the armed struggle; my sister, whom I love, also desisted. I had "effective" examples of who made different decisions.'

How did the rational decision you are talking about mature?

'You see, I worked for 10 years at CAM, a subsidiary of Italsider, fighting for a reduction in working hours and to get a canteen. I eventually worked full time for the union as a union representative. Yes, I knew that many workers had two jobs and that they were using me, but I was glad to be used because I was working for a worthwhile cause: the cause of dignified and more human labour, for a better quality of life. At that time I had not yet joined any group.'

You see what I am telling you, you achieved a lot, accomplished many 'bits of your cause' without killing anyone. So was it possible to fight without killing?

'It was violent action anyway, and without such violence you do not obtain anything; violence has to be answered with violence, there is no other way. At that time there was a good deal of violence, between groups of the extreme left and Fascists, between extra-parliamentary groups and the police. I might well have died, as might a Fascist or a policeman have. In a word, violence was taken for granted and my choice of armed struggle was connected to all that. You know that Mara Cagol, Renato Curcio's wife, who died in an armed clash with the Carabinieri in June 1975 and who founded the Red Brigades, sought alternative solutions to direct violence, but she did not find them. And then violence is part of man; you as a psychologist know that.'

Certainly, but it is part of man's maturing process to symbolise and represent violence, in order to avoid implementing it. We are not hydraulic systems, faucets, but rather symbolising animals and it is much more human to keep the struggle alive by keeping your adversary alive, precisely in order that he may in the end recognise your 'spiritual' superiority, rather than to eliminate him, that is, to eliminate the struggle and in the final analysis to eliminate everything that on the part of the other may arouse anger and anxiety. Through violence we come to speak of death: can you tell me how you could truly justify killing an enemy?

'I never killed anyone; perhaps I let people be killed – although I will never know that. I did not "sing" after I was arrested and did not say where the comrades of Cinisello were, not even after a year in solitary confinement. In any case I never considered myself a murderer; we had declared war on the State, even though the State did not recognise us as combatants. In this context people were killed, were kidnapped and died, and we were arrested and stripped of our dignity in prison. No, there was no affective justification of a personal kind. We killed people we did not know except for the fact that they were opponents, class enemies. It was unpleasant to kill, the thought of the relatives of the victims brought us suffering, but it was necessary for a higher cause, and what I am most sorry about is that the dead on both sides died in vain, because the choice of armed struggle, which at the time seemed to us the last hurdle, was certainly a lost cause.'

The State did not kill you, even though the militants in the armed struggle did kill.

'No, I surrendered, a basic right in war. You do not kill people who surrender; I put up my hands. Bear in mind, however, that the State kills in any case if it finds itself in a situation where its survival seems threatened.

The choice of armed struggle rather than political struggle depends on the level of class conflict: both from the extent of class conflict and from the goals that the group thinks that it wants and must seek. During all my militancy it never seemed justified or acceptable to me that anyone should die during a robbery; it was not conceivable that an official of Mondialpol or a passer-by should die in an action, but in an armed clash several deaths might have seemed legitimate in order to free political prisoners.

Because to free those prisoner comrades who had worked out the political policy of the armed struggle meant ensuring the continuation of our programme, while in making expropriations we were just satisfying our needs for survival.'

What was most gratifying about your militancy?

I do not know how to answer that. They needed me and I let myself be used. I was satisfied with that. Regarding the question you already asked F, whether she felt herself diminished as a woman, no, I did not feel myself denaturised. It is true what F said about Silveria Russo, that is, that she was a soldier, but we were all soldiers, the men too.'

How did your distancing yourself from the armed struggle come about? Was it a question of a rational decision, of moral qualms, of losing hope?

'I had myself arrested. I went back home precisely so that the Digos [Division for General Investigations of the National Police] would become aware of me. That they would arrest me sooner or later was on the cards. I was disgusted with the base motives – that is, the psychological motives – of many comrades who had taken up the armed struggle and with the power struggles within the Red Brigades caused by the distorting effect of power on the minds of leaders and followers: for example, a comrade's escape was not organised for fear of losing power to him.'

In other words, the principal reason these comrades had for belonging to the armed struggle was their sense of their own importance and the cause was something that served their purposes rather than that they were serving the cause. This could explain or make it possible to understand two conflicting attitudes, the over-ready repentance of some, who as you

**yourself told me, after 7 years of killing told everything in 2
seconds, and the extreme toughness of women like BPA who still
kept a sense of their own greatness by refusing to give in.**

'I think you are right. In any case it is all connected. I had a great
many arguments in prison with women who wanted to become preg-
nant to get better treatment. The child was theirs and they used it as
they had previously used weapons. But a child is not a pistol and
should not be used like a weapon as a means of violence, just as, after
the armed struggle had failed, they used penitentism to keep from dying in prison. At that point I have to ask myself whether they could
even reach the point of using a child as a weapon for the "continuation of life". Well, an idea like that seems to me, and has always
seemed to me, to be aberrant. You cannot dedicate your life to achieving a better quality of life for everyone and then exclude your own
child from this programme of happiness for everyone.'

**Let us go back, if you do not mind, to your distancing yourself
from the armed struggle.**

'I have been made to figure in the category of penitents. As it happened, I never claimed to be a prisoner of war. I confirmed everything my comrades accused me of after they were arrested. I never
collaborated before that despite the fact that disinformation had made
my name appear among those of the penitents of the moment. I did
not think it wise to make a decision for the comrades who were still
out, since I thought they were sane enough and of age to decide what
to do with their own lives and their own decisions. My faith is not
dead, however, quite the contrary. I consider Communism beyond men,
beyond penitents, beyond people who have dissociated themselves and
people who do not yield. You see, I do not believe in a rigid distinction between penitentism, dissociation and obduracy. In my opinion
the distinctions are contrived. Moral penitence may exist, but prison
has a more important impact on penitentism: you are stripped of your
dignity and then you have to survive. Sentiment also plays a part: ties
with relatives, a fiancé, etc. My child's father is a penitent.'

What is penitentism for you?

'A nightmarish reaction to a nightmarish event.'

Appendix 4: Joint Meeting with Mara Aldrovandi and Mario Ferrandi, 2 April 1990

1.
In your opinion do men join the armed struggle for the same reasons as women?

He – I can tell you that women would not have put Moro on trial. There is a kind of political cynicism that only men have. In Potere Operaio (Worker Power) we were not anti-feminist, but we took into consideration attitudes toward combat and command when it was a question of choosing a woman to work with. Sex did not enter into it at all at that point. Women are moralists, with a visceral kind of moralism that history, at any rate, is not made with: in practice, women take part in the armed struggle because of all the violence they have suffered.

She – Women have been robbed by political cynicism. I have suffered a good deal of violence and so have all women, but I never had the nerve to make myself an executioner of the night like you, Ferrandi. I have to admit that Worker Avant-garde gave a good deal of opportunity to women. It is obvious that a Communist ought not to discriminate against women. I like the adventure of feminism, but I do not like little self-important islands. At the Borletti plant there were many comrades who were disrespectful toward women, but the women succeeded in making them stop. Sex has nothing to do with ability to command. In an illegal organisation there is no place for the feminist question.

2.
In your opinion do men repent for the same reasons as women?

He – Offhand I would say yes. You become a penitent quickly or you do not become one at all. You have to take into consideration the need for a false conscience in many penitents and people who have dissociated. Whether you have been driven to that decision by your own personal fragility or fooled into doing it, a fatal defence mechanism is triggered within you to find a noble justification. That is a responsibility that reflects on the magistrates.

She – When you wind up in jail you care only about finding comrades. Prison is very efficient in rebuilding webs of friendship and affective relationships. I met four idiots who had no moral sense or anything. At that point I really have to say, better ordinary women than political ones of that kind! In any event it is not that women are more or less capable of being penitent than men; it depends on how they carried on the armed struggle.

3.
Have you ever been afraid of the vengeance of former comrades?

He – Yes, but it was a calculated risk. I was beaten up too. But it was my own fault. They came looking for me. My reaction to those who tried to make it look as if I had been kicked out was to become more determined and obstinate.

She – As far as I am concerned, those who want to give you a beating because you sang have got psychological problems. I am not afraid of revenge, though I know there are people with sick minds. They made threatening telephone calls to me for a year.

4.
Was there anything in your experience in the armed struggle that you miss?

He – No longer being able to unmask the hypocrisy of those in power, a hypocrisy of a completely servile kind. That should not be something characteristic only of the armed struggle. We wanted to expose the inconsistencies through a show of action. I greatly missed a powerful agency for social action.

She – The collectivity. The group supported you. However, in the armed struggle one could only discuss particular events; you could not bring your feelings into it. It was not enjoyable being in the armed struggle; it was our duty.

5.
In your opinion has the State done anything to resolve on the political level and not just the penal level, the explosive tensions that brought on the armed struggle?

He – The State has not addressed this problem itself, but I doubt that it is a matter for the State. I think that this is a problem for some others who have always believed in the theory of a double truth: now we are in one mode, when the right moment comes we will be in another. This double truth or double morality is something that had done us all in. If anything, it is the State's business to eliminate everything that makes marginalising easier, like whatever completely blocks one's own creative potential.

She – Perhaps only individuals have tried to change the situations that are the source of social tensions. The PCI, which should examine its conscience in greater depth, has not yet owned up to its responsibilities.

Appendix 5: Joint Meeting with Mara Aldrovandi and Mario Ferrandi, 7 April 1990

Mario Ferrandi's political militancy began in 1973 in Worker Power and 2 years later he made the choice of armed struggle, like the greater part of his group. The discussion between him and Mara heated up precisely over this brief period between legal militancy and illegal militancy. Keep in mind that Mara took 10 years before entering armed struggle from Worker Avant-garde, where she acted as a union representative and she is at pains to emphasise that she never acted as an 'executioner of the night' (that is, Mara never killed).

How is it that you never killed during your armed militancy?

'By chance', answers Mara.
   Mario Ferrandi confirms that many who are alive are not dead only by chance.

'Those who join the armed struggle too fast', Mara objects, 'cannot have had the time to experience the failure of peaceful avenues and so they went into armed struggle and, hence, into the possibility of killing, without a sufficient level of conscience.'

SM said in a conversation with me, which I cannot report as an interview, that political homicide is acceptable. Everything depends on the conscience with which you act. Do you agree with this evaluation?

'Yes, I agree. Ethics and politics are all one. But politics says that it is first necessary to sensitise the persons near you, to wait for base legitimation and to see that there are really no alternatives. And there were no alternatives!', rebuts Mara very passionately. 'As a woman I suffered a good deal of violence from individuals who, however, reflected in their behaviour the negative values of a male-oriented society: the society was violent, and so its guardians, the police, were violent; my employer was violent, not by using physical violence, but by not respecting the rights of the workers; the male workers were violent when they put photographs of nude women in their lockers. At a certain point one says that's enough. There was no proportion at all between the violence of the state and ours!'

'That's right', responds Mario Ferrandi, 'There was no proportion: even if 100 state officials were bad. That still does not mean that we are under a dictatorship. Yours is a visceral moralism, Mara, and history does not get made with moralisms!'

'I am amazed that you of all people, with your history, should say these things!', she objects.

'I have repented for my moralism. We did indeed think of ourselves as night executioners. I killed a drug dealer and I sensed a certain sympathy in the police who arrested us. However, we set ourselves up as criminals and we paid the consequences of it. If you set yourself up as a national army of liberation, you must respect the rules of the Geneva Convention, which means not killing civilians, for example, and we did that. . . .'

'We have talked a lot, however, about the Moro case!', responds Mara.

'Almost not at all', rebuts Mario.

Do you think that that was not fighting honourably?

'No, no military ethic was ever promulgated', Mario replies.

'It is unacceptable to kill a prisoner after such a long detention. We applied what the angry citizen asks for every once in a while: the death penalty. They could not consider us political prisoners because we set ourselves up as criminals with a double morality: we can kidnap all the Moros we want, but we must take advantage of the guarantees that the State offers. I say that as Communists we should have given an example of greater humanity and instead we did worse than our adversaries. And what is worse is that we fell into the trap set for us by the P2 Lodge: the massacre of Piazza Fontana, the massacre of the Italicus train, were prepared on an *ad hoc* basis to drive a certain part of the movement of the left toward terrorism and to crystallize public opinion against it. We fell for it.'

'No', object Mara, 'I am not a product of Piazza Fontana'.

Perhaps you fell into it because if one becomes aware of a really dangerous situation, the best defence against fear is active participation. You acted in the manner you thought the most efficacious possible. This played into the hands of secret powers, as you call them. . . .

Mario agrees and adds, 'There might have been an alternative: we could have joined the Carabinieri and the magistracy and occupied the nerve centres of power and changed it profoundly through a different kind of presence within it, because "it is one thing to feed a fire and another to put it out".'

'It is you, Mara, who did not see any alternative! In any event the Communist Party had a great responsibility for this because it taught people to deviate from morality and ethics, persuading them to adopt a double morality and this led to a tragic watershed.'

'Anyway, in this watershed of a double ethics or as we might say of no ethics, we thought that killing only those who had serious personal responsibilities was justified. We killed a drug dealer, for example. Lotta Continua (Continuous Struggle) performed the first political murder: the Calabresi murder. You must know that there was a committee against State massacres that the Red Brigades, Dario Fo and Feltrinelli also belonged to. Perhaps Sofri himself did not give the order but. . . . We found ourselves with an armed struggle that was spreading in 1976/7, one that had a vigilante character. And when a point is reached where killing proletarians is justified because they are drunk, with the gall to brag about it (three friends of mine killed some drunk workers who tried to throw them out of a bar; they were armed and shot them . . .), you can see that with the double ethics you have deceived yourself. I should have reported these comrades to the command so that it could judge them, but it did not seem worthwhile to me and I went to England.'

(Before the group meeting began Mario Ferrandi had talked a lot about England and, above all, about English prisons: prison guards are trained to respect the dignity of man, even though prison conditions are harsher than in Italy. In any case two centuries of democracy there have affected the criminal system too: policemen do not shoot and neither do the thieves. Here relations are much rougher and more brutal.)

'The armed struggle,' says Mario, 'was a powerful therapeutic and socialising agency where each individual could feel influential in resolving social and family problems. Something like a cooperative, which, however, it was not.'

'It did not matter if you were handsome or ugly, young or old, and we changed our names and that was cathartic. For many of us it was a culture, even though that ought not to be a particular characteristic of the armed struggle.'

'We studied the works of Marx and Lenin,' Mara notes.

'As compared with that experience', says Mario, 'today I miss not being able to unmask the hypocrisy of the powerful as we were doing then and the subservience of the press. Before I had some effect, but not any longer now.'

'For me,' says Mara, 'it is the collective aspect that I miss most, the fact that I was not alone, that I was accepted and could talk about everything. This was true, however, only of my militancy before the armed struggle, because in the armed struggle I could only talk about fliers and goals.'

Mario continues: 'And the State did everything except take responsibility for the problems, the tensions that were at the bottom of the armed struggle and which made it explode. Individual people did it, perhaps individual magistrates. There are those who are respectful and humane, and who try to understand and then a dialogue begins on this . . . but there are those who try to get around you with crooked methods because they want to get ahead and bring home a penitent. I think this is a serious fault that reflects entirely on the magistrates. I have seen people totally short-circuited. You have to keep in mind the personalities you are dealing with and how you use them.'

'Perhaps they ought to employ consultants,' Mara suggests.

'I cannot take for granted a democracy that does not exist, by considering collaboration something natural, I mean. Many penitents have been beaten. But in any case I must applaud the judges who kept the phenomenon of the armed struggle from ending for its authors in the Argentine manner, that is, with "desaparecidos".'

'I agree', Mara confirms, 'but it is not just to the credit of the judges. It was also the veneer of democracy that this country has which would not permit a legitimation of the phenomenon of the "desaparecidos" in the court of public opinion.'

Let us come now to the question of repentance.

'You have to be careful when you appraise "penitence"', says Mario. 'You know there is a great need for a false conscience in many penitents and those who have dissociated. When you are driven to that decision by your personal fragility or you are fooled into doing it, a fatal defence mechanism comes into play, fatal for oneself, in order to give oneself a noble justification.'

By minimising the action, perhaps, by saying that it is just a matter of manipulating the judges and that it is not exactly a matter of what one has done.

'Exactly,' replies Mario. 'But in any case as far as what you are interested in is concerned, I would say off-hand that there is no difference between a man's penitence and a woman's, except that women repent viscerally and, hence, experience a good many conflicts, whereas for men penitence is an art.'

'Of course it is an art, just as for a man all life is a continual performance,' adds Mara. 'I repented, if we want to use that term, because in the name of what was I supposed to do 15 years in prison, now that there was no longer any motivation whatever for armed struggle, much less for prison. Instead I got myself arrested. And then it was by chance that I did not become a hard-core non-collaborationist, because I did not end up in Palmi where my world would have been limited to just my obdurate comrades and only with them "would I have felt and desired", as Betti Pasqua Aurora says. Don't underestimate prison and its effects on people.'

'In my repentance there was a plan', says Mario, 'one that perhaps was not very clear from the beginning, but one that was followed with ever greater stubbornness every time they tried to turn me into an outcast, which is more important than punishing you when they are dealing with obduracy. I even took a beating once, but it was a calculated risk and anyway I consider myself capable of judging pretty well the danger my former comrades were in and my own too.

'To go back to my plan, for me repentance was a very good thing because it destroyed the idea of a moral consistency for the sake of which one sacrifices others and oneself. Those accused of terrorism who repented found that the Church, which understands betrayal as an aspect of being human and which expects inconsistency, welcomed them. Honour, faithfulness and discipline are a Fascist inheritance and are not suited to man. Penitentism made it possible not to be prisoners of an abstract idea about consistency: to give way is normal, daily life is not heroic. There is the crux of the matter that has to be faced.'

With regard to repentance, Mara, do you think that women are more open to the idea than men, or less?

'To judge feminine repentance you have to begin with one's joining the armed struggle, which for women is something much more thought over than for men, because women have more at stake than men', responds Mara.

'I am sure that for a woman giving up motherhood is terrible, the idea of not marrying because there is no time for it is terrible. A man does not have motherhood at stake. In a word, women think it over three times before joining the armed struggle.

'And as far as male repentance is concerned, as Mario Ferrandi has just told you, I think there is a good amount of uneasy conscience there. I have never heard a man say: "Comrades, I couldn't go on", which is what does happen, because one cannot resist psychological pressure, sometimes physical too, perhaps even torture.

'In the armed struggle women had to win equality because, and let us not forget it, violence has always been masculine and women have always been subjected to it.'

I tell Mara and Mario about the matriarchal dominion hypothesised by Bachofen before the advent of patriarchy and about the fact that on the 13th day of the 13th month of the lunar year the male divine coadjutor [*paredros*] was killed by the women companions of the great priestess of the Great Mother; either by a cannibalistic act of these same priestesses or by being torn to pieces or by being thrown off a cliff....

'But could he have chosen not to?', smiles Mara.

Appendix 6: Silveria Russo, 16 March 1990 – Questionnaire

1.
What were the family relationships in your original family? Do you have a favourable recollection of your family?

Yes, my parents never made me go without anything. If I have painful memories they do not regard intrafamily life but the situation of the whole family, which had to leave its familiar social and urban surroundings of Bologna to transfer to Turin, in surroundings completely different. Yes, that is a memory that is particularly painful.

Have you ever idealised one of your parents or a substitute for one of them?

Yes, my father. I idealised more than loved him. He criticised the Communist Party left; he saw in it the worker who wanted to become middle class. He was a Communist and a Catholic. Many of us have Communist and Catholic origins. Segio and Bignami were children of partisans. Bignami's father was a person who did not want to give up his weapons.

Did you ever have the feeling that you were deprived of something vital, something very important, in your childhood, that you were lacking something that it was your right to have?

No, not in my family. In my political training, yes. I, along with many others, missed the Communist Party as a putative father who never wanted to recognise us as his children. It behaved toward us in a schizophrenic way.

I would like to know how you felt about belonging to the armed struggle with regard to family dynamics. In opposition? (For example, the family did not want to discuss social problems and class struggle.)

No, quite the opposite.

As a continuation? (The armed struggle manifests at society level what has already been experienced in a conflictual family situation.)

No.

As an escape? (Better the armed struggle than the family.)

No.

2.
Tell me about your reasons for joining Prima Linea. It is not really the political analysis that interests me, unless you want to go over it. I am curious above all to know what feelings led you to join the armed struggle: love of the cause?

No.

Dedication to a cause out of deep conviction as to its rightness?

It was a personal decision: a responsibility to be taken on. We felt like vigilantes. Prima Linea came into being that way, out of a group of friends who used to meet in a bar in Sesto and wanted to be Robin Hoods.

A sense of your own greatness and/or of your own importance?

It was a question of that for some of the big penitents, but not for us.

3.
What was the occasion of your joining the armed struggle?

(a) Group friendships?

Yes. I looked for Lotta Continua [Continuous Struggle] and I helped found Prima Linea. From Continuous Struggle [Silveria Russo remained in Continuous Struggle until 1973] I brought the feminist argument about uniting the personal and the political into Prima Linea. GB also agreed with this argument.

(b) I was selected because I was already a sympathiser?

No.

(c) I still do not understand what brought it about?

I cannot imagine why we got to thinking that way. It was a schizo-phrenic way of thinking influenced by ideology. It was mad.

4.
What justified the killing of an enemy for you?

(a) It was necessary for the cause but I felt badly about it?

Yes, but it was a schizophrenia between sentiment and reason, be-tween the desire to live in peace and to feel like part of a movement. But you see the schizophrenia was of the group, not just mine. Only if you appreciate this side of it can you understand it. . . . And then there were some who did not have a reason but only a confused feeling. One like that was more vulnerable to making extreme choices in a moment of crisis concerning the question of solidarity.

(b) He was an oppressor or a symbol of oppression or one who worked zealously for those in power?

Yes, and so we did not feel guilty. We killed with the logic of a war, one which, however, we had declared all by ourselves. Even so, it was only permissible to kill certain persons in accordance with particular rules. A magistrate was not to be killed if he was with his wife and daughter. We killed those who were guilty of grave deeds, like the psychiatrist of the Collegno hospital, who tortured patients to make them behave, and the engineer of Icmesa. We never killed, as certain print media have said, by choosing matchsticks out of a bunch, in other words at random.

(c) Nothing justified the killing of an enemy?

5.
What, above all, did the armed struggle mean for you?

(a) Annihilation of the oppressors?

(b) Creation of a more just society?

The more just society that we wanted to establish was not a Commu-nist one with a single party. It was a truly democratic society with power in the hands of Soviets, one that perhaps would have pleased Gorbachev. We had an ideology of a vigilante counter-power, which is in fact workerism. We were against Marxism–Leninism and its concept of the party as the avant-garde of the proletariat. Our programme had its roots in the Communist disagreement of the twenties, that is, it was along the lines of the opposition of Pannckoek and Luxemburg to 'Leninism', and it was developed by certain fringe groups of Potere Operaio (Worker Power), by the fringe group of Scalzone (not those of Negri and Tronti), which wanted to take a position between German Marxism (Spartacus League: all power to the councils) and Leninism. Our idea did not provide for the organisation of an avant-garde in the party but counter-proposed a self-organisation of the class in Italy in councils. This matter of self-organisation is a fundamental one, because it differentiates the various traditions that the armed groups came from. The Red Brigades favoured a party structured in a strongly hierarchical way, and they were in fact a rough copy of Marxism–Leninism. It is also important to know that our programme had an evangelical Utopia as its matrix, one pushed to the limit certainly. At this point a whole argument could be developed, one that I am concerned with in a particularly intense way, about Catholic opposition between the sixties and the seventies, which the conciliar demands themselves made definite, and which set itself to dealing with reality with a logic that was equally 'institutional' although of an opposite brand. These were the theories. The theories had these particular ideological references, which perhaps did not have real references. We took the proletarians of San Basilio as nothing less than the first example of making the working class independent!

6.
If armed struggle was supposed to create a world founded on justice, did you consider yourselves the direct artificers of this creation or its instruments? (Have you ever felt that it could not have been done differently?)

We were convinced that we could not act differently, that we had to use violence; there was no room for anything else. I said this to the feminists of Turin too, who had made a non-violent choice that would have been a normal choice for a woman.

7.
Were there moments when you had doubts about the armed struggle or were you always in symbiosis with it?

After Via Millio. This was true of my husband too. It was terrible to have killed the student Iurilli. He died by chance because he happened to be there. This brought on a deep crisis for some comrades, some of whom, like Donat Cattin, went abroad. We, however, decided to remain. There were comrades in prison to be freed: they were more important for us than they were for the Red Brigades.

8.
What was there about your militancy that most gratified you?

(a) A sense of defiance of society?

I most liked using firearms. With them we could be intransigent toward society and we could be of importance within the group.

(b) Human relationships within the group?

We – the B woman, the Azzaroni woman and I – always tried to make a case for combining the personal and the political. From this discussion there resulted among other things the decision about the zealous and repressive woman guard as a test for the feminists (the woman guard was only wounded). It was an argument that did not have and could not have any chance in an illegal organisation.
   Hence, there was conflict in intragroup relations as well.

(c) Interchangeability of roles? Both women and men can shoot and kill, both women and men can be heads of logistical and operational networks?

There were some, but we had to insist on them. It was not a rule that the distribution of tasks should be done in that way.

9.
Did you ever feel tension between your femininity and belonging to an armed group? Did the experience you had enrich you or did you feel that you had to give up a part of yourself? Having listened to the interviews with women who were former

**terrorists on 'Notte della Repubblica', I got the impression that
there was a kind of hardening of the women comrades. Can you
confirm or deny this impression?**

There was a good deal of separation between personal life and militant life. This was true for everybody, but above all for women, who
had to give up their children, at least unless they made an irresponsi-
ble decision. If there was the hardening you speak of, it came from
wanting to be taken seriously. Women found a kind of liberation in
armed militancy.

**Did devotion to the cause strengthen a man's love for his own
woman comrade? Was he proud that his companion fought
alongside him?**

**10.
What did distancing yourself from the armed struggle mean?**

(a) Would you describe it as an emotional feeling?

Yes. The episode of Via Millio shocked us a great deal. It was contrary to the rules of war which envisage deaths among the enemy and
possible deaths of militants but not accidental deaths like the one of
the student Iurilli.

**(b) A rational decision? (I want to survive, now that it is all
over and make plans for the future?)**

Yes, I want to survive and give testimony of my mistakes. The testimony of the dissociating path I have taken is the only message I can
send to the relatives of the victims.

(c) Moral uneasiness?

Yes, but public contrition is useless.

(d) Desperation?

No, I do not suffer from the 'ashes-on-the-head' syndrome. I do not
want to be devastated by a sense of guilt and I do not want to commit
suicide. I would instead very much like to get back to voting again to

return to an active participation, which now makes much more sense to me than before. I do not want to be sorry either for having been born. But I have in any case a very clear idea of my limitations. My active choice would be an anonymous one. But I think it would be a mistake to erase the historical memory of it. I intend to establish a consulting agency of my own for the training of personnel in the field of social services. There is a good market for it here in Bergamo. And above everything, there is a need to establish in a psychological and social sense a culture of solidarity in which we workers in the field of services can make our wealth of experience fruitful.

11.
Why the cooperation with the justice system?

Unanswered.

12.
If you had to describe your former comrades' naming you as an accomplice, what would you call it?

Informing, destroying solidarity. But the subject is complex. First of all jail is a slaughterhouse; there were Red Brigades who fuelled the atmosphere of suspicion. We were absolutely against this kind of atmosphere though we harboured suspicions whenever the situation was not immediately clear to everyone (for example, the milder treatment of a prisoner or the sudden, unexpected visit of a judge) and particularly with regard to movements of our comrades from one prison to another. When we suspected or knew someone had yielded, we tried to understand the reasons. This, of course, was made more difficult by the spread of suspicion, that is, the ones we suspected, suspected us too as their probable judges. After imprisonment many of the penitents did not want to see one another again, but this regarded those who became dissociated as well. Perhaps the difference was in the fact that we tried to keep up mutual respect and tried not to argue in front of our inquisitors.

13.
How did you feel about the police who caught you and the judges who tried you?

When I got to know them I saw that there were some among them that one could talk to and with whom it was worthwhile to be in communication.

14.
Did the armed struggle leave behind any possibility of a cultural legacy or just a lot of pain?

Both. We can only give testimony about the path of our own life and faith. Public penitentism shows little respect for the pain of the relatives of the victims. The armed struggle has perhaps left a historical memory that can be transformed into political wisdom. As I have already told you, I would like to carry into society my share of political wisdom.

15.
What things do you now consider important in your life?

The family, my son, my university studies [political science in Bologna]. I am writing a thesis on the political ideas of Dossetti. I feel very close to Catholic thought, though certainly not to Communion and Liberation.

I am also going to specialise. My son is staying with my parents who have really given me a great deal of help. I like to stay at home during breaks, because I can spend a little more time with Gabriele who is two and a half years old.

16.
Is there anything in your life that you would like me to ask you about?

The importance that a certain over-emphasis on an evangelical Utopia had relative to joining the armed struggle.

[On this, see the third interview granted by Silveria Russo and Bruno Laronga – see pp. 157–65.]

Any questions of the interviewee for the interviewer?

There are apparently no explicit or implied questions that Silveria Russo wishes to express. We will give her the benefit of the doubt.

[Notes concerning the interview.]

Very forthcoming but careful that her memory not be 'falsified' or misinterpreted, that everything be done with respect for persons and for the level of communication. The *leitmotif* of the interview was to find the greatest possible continuity between life before and after, a thing that is very easy for her.

She is aware in the psychological appraisement of her feminine experience in the armed struggle of how it differs from a male experience.

Appendix 7: Joint Meeting with Silveria Russo and Bruno Laronga, Bergamo, 16 March 1990

Silveria Russo is a beautiful woman, well-groomed and well-dressed, with an open smile. She is 40 years old but seems much younger. The meeting took place in the 'Cooperative Monte Rosso' where Silveria works on probation (under articles 48, 50 of the Penitentiary Regulations). For her, in contrast to the situation of Ettorina Zaccheo, there are no legal problems with giving interviews.

At the beginning there is just the two of us. Her husband will join us after about 2 hours. He had the benefit of the law of 1987 on dissociation and is now serving 22 years in prison.

Besides her work-release status under article 48, she enjoys leaves awarded (under article 52) as a mother (taking care of affective interests) and for study (she has re-enrolled in political science).

She was in Continuous Struggle and a feminist, but was critical of the feminist movement because it divided the personal from the political and eschewed violence. Before Continuous Struggle she had a full political career: in 1966 she was in Catholics in Dissent, which subsequently 'yielded in order to carry on a class discussion'. She joined 'Quaderni Rossi' [Red Notebooks]. Subsequently, in 1969, she was in Continuous Struggle, and at the end of the road there was Prima Linea.

The feminist debate became obsolete for her beginning in 1975, when Prima Linea did not yet exist; it was created in 1976 by a 'group of zealots from the suburbs who met in a bar in Sesto and intended to act as vigilantes, as Robin Hoods'. Silveria brought the feminist discussion on combining the personal with the political into Prima Linea, supported in this by the woman comrade B, but she found little acceptance for it. The men thought that it was an element of distortion

to think about how to humanise war, that is, to give it a feminine
character. B and Silveria were 'pushed aside into logistics'.

**Where was this personal that you wanted to combine with the
political?**

The personal was nowhere. I was not there like a single person, unique
and unrepeatable, as you say. I was there in the name of an ideology
that motivated me, as the representative of a movement; it was unfortunate that often it was a case of my projections on what was the
reality.

**'It seems to me', I say to Silveria, 'that humanising the war
means going in search of the Uroboros, putting opposites
together and that this too is an operation that involves expelling
everything bad so that within the group there may be only what
is good.'**

'You are right', says Silveria, 'at that point we ought to have seen
that it was not easy to achieve. This discussion began again with the
COLP [Comunisti Organizzati per la Liberazione Proletaria – Organised Communists for Proletarian Liberation]. All the leadership cadres
had been arrested, that is, those who planned and conducted operations, these leadership cadres being all men. The women who carried
on support and informational activities – except for a few, among whom
I, Ronconi and R [Silveria belonged to the national intelligence command while Ronconi belonged to the national command] remained
untouched by the great arrests. So the COLP forces were directed principally by women, who reopened the debate on political murder and
tried to strengthen cohesion and solidarity between our male and female comrades. In other words, the COLP put the group back into
shape in terms of solidarity. The activities of the COLP were principally robberies for internal financing and to finance the escape of
imprisoned comrades. The escape of Susanna Ronconi was organised
by them and by the Nuclei Operativi [Operational Units] of Segio Sergio.
That is why there was less penitentism (loss of solidarity, informing):
those women who had had a planning and operational role, those who
had tried to combine the personal with the political, "repented" much
less. However, this was also true of the men: those who had only
feelings or only rationality were more prone to repent in an atmosphere of failing solidarity and of informing, at a time of crisis in the

values of solidarity. Prison played an important role in causing penitentism: prison then was a slaughterhouse and many retractions came
out of fear. We were always against considering the person who was
"actively dissociated" as just a scoundrel and a villain: in the end the
penitents were useful to us too in dissociating ourselves, that is, for
the purposes of rethinking our history critically.'

[*Bruno Laronga joins us in the discussion. It is about 12:30.*]

'Rethinking', says Silveria, 'is not something that we alone need to
do. The unconditional glorification of the Resistance also ought to be
rethought: there too there were acts of terrorism, but they cannot be
talked about. The Communist Party has finally distanced itself from
Togliatti, from Marxism–Leninism, in the sense that it has now brought
its image into line with what it had already practiced.'

**Perhaps it is precisely the victims it strewed around that gives
the State and the political class today an excuse for not thinking
about their own violence.**

Certainly.

**Projecting onto others, seeing in them only the evil that you have
done yourself, as the State has done, as the Communist Party has
done. Think too about the state of mind of those policemen who
know that you consider them enemies, scoundrels and servants
of the State and who hence have to defend themselves more than
they have to defend the State and are perhaps full of resentment
toward you, the same resentment you have within you.**

'Our way of thinking', says Silveria, 'was schizophrenic, split between
the reason that produced the ideology and the feelings with which,
when the chosen victim was with his wife and child, we went home
without striking and used to strike when he was alone in order not to
terrify the family. It was group schizophrenia, however, not personal,
even though it also had personal repercussions. This schizophrenia was
also a question of being young, a generational matter.'

Was joining the group like looking for a new family?

We experienced it in Prima Linea, others experienced it in the scouts;
its manifestations were various. Many did indeed look for a new family,
seeking perhaps those elements of identity that were lacking in the

family. This goes back to the split between parents and children in our original families, in that our families had certain orientations; we were the fruits of an Italy that was changing, and so we needed to find outside our families those elements of identity that we needed to grow and to deal with reality.

Was it facing reality or your own ideas of reality?

'That is the way it always is,' responds Bruno, 'you are always dealing with ideas of reality. So I would not be so sure that it was a matter of growth. How can you talk about growth when on the basis of schizophrenic ideas we end up in a group of schizophrenics? I do not recognise myself very much in Silveria's definition of our relationship with the external world and with ourselves. I am hanging on to my idea of dispensing justice. I do not consider myself a child of anyone, and I am not a child of an Italy that is changing. I wanted to save the workers from their oppression by a system oriented toward profit and not toward service.'

Once the decision about an armed group had been made, did any code of honour in fighting exist?

'Yes,' responds Bruno, 'death was handed out with a good many doubts. A war code was needed; there were many deaths at the hands of people without honour. For us, only territorially distributed violence was justified, the kind linked to social needs. I was always very careful in preparing the conditions so that there might not be accidents along the way, so that no more violence than necessary would be used. Unfortunately the unexpected can always happen in a war situation.

'Iurilli stepped in my way, the bank messenger stepped in MR's way. In any case I did not aim on purpose and I am sure that if I had not been wounded in the hand and arm, as I was, that student would not have died. After the "exponential" power of Via Fani, everybody would want to repeat in his own neighbourhood a kind of violence that has no connection with the violence of "the masses". We were not strong enough to oppose that initiative.'

Did you agree with there being female commands in Prima Linea?

'Women's violence was just a desire for prominence. No, I was not in agreement, and I was a fool to permit the wounding of the woman prison guard.'

Appendix 8: Joint Meeting with Silveria Russo and Bruno Laronga, 9 April 1990

1.
In your opinion did men join the armed struggle for the same reasons as women?

He – I think the motives may have been similar. Except that women had an additional one, that of being emancipated. Without any doubt their way of being in the armed struggle was different: there was no female commander and in any case aptitude for command is masculine. Women had a place: or if they did not have one right away they took one, but they had trouble enunciating a political plan of their own. Our political plan went by way of the myth of a union between the intellectual and the political.

Women lacked ready initiative, the strength to lead; the distribution of tasks turned out to be detrimental to women. However, in determination they were even superior to us men. As the representative of the Walter Alasia group I met one woman, Betti Pasqua Aurora, who had determination enough to beat everyone!

She – No, because their psychology is different. Women have more strength, more sense of solidarity.'

2.
In your opinion do men repent for the same reasons as women?

He – I have always thought that women are stronger. They gave more thought both to engaging in the armed struggle and to repenting. And I am convinced that violence is not feminine. And then there are women like FB who had more responsibilities than their actual psychological involvement, especially regarding the political growth that they were able to foster within the group. But this is true of men also, for example, as regards V, who was psychologically a kind of hired killer. In any case he had a special relationship with SS, not with us.

She – The women sublimated crises with efforts at solidarity. In every crisis they knew how to bring the men and women together. And then there may be personal reasons for repentance.

There can be a personality structure that predisposes one for less resistance to stressful events like vaginal examinations in prison, the fact that you were allowed only 1 hour out in the fresh air, that the surveillance on you was of a particularly persecutory character. Faced with these circumstances, I never gave any indication of yielding, nor did persons who might perhaps seem vulnerable, like CZ.

Female physiology is a particular problem relative to a woman's resistance in prison: you stop feeling like a women because you menstruate less frequently, as happened to T.

3.
Have you ever been afraid of the vengeance of former comrades?

He – We made a collective decision. Dissociation was our last collective decision.

She – Fear was instilled by the BR [Red Brigades], not by us.

4.
Was there anything in your experience in the armed struggle that you miss?

He – The troop a little bit, the chance to face danger together. The disinterestedness of our relations, our honesty. Today you always see a selfish angle. It was nice in Prima Linea: we knew how to make a distinction between human errors and wilful errors; the Red Brigades did not.

It never interested me to have someone tell me about his mistakes unless they were wilful mistakes.

She – No, I do not miss anything. I am only sorry I did not get my head straightened out earlier. I would have preferred not to have engaged in the armed struggle and, hence, also not to do 10 years in prison, even though I matured in prison. Yes, you could also grow in prison. I am sorry that a person like Betti Pasqua Aurora did not learn anything in prison and is still there being obdurate, that is, being an equestrian statue.

5.

**n your opinion has the State done anything to resolve at the
political level and not just at the penal level, the explosive
tensions that brought on the armed struggle?**

He – The Italian Government has seen the defeat of the Communist
Party as the working class's defining moment. Before there was an
ambition to have power. Now we no longer know what power is. Capital
has been very clever in destroying the class make-up of Italian society. In 1980 there was a definitive loss of Marxism as a critical
force. So it may be said that the state has tried to dissolve every possible attack force against Italy's economic and political set-up.

What has specifically been done for the relatives of the victims is
another matter: the State has not done anything to make it psychologically possible to get over that period because it has not permitted any
catharsis, which is what happens at the end of a war both for the
winners and the losers. The State has never recognised our war and so
the relatives of the victims cannot even get a feeling of the death of
their dear ones.

The armed struggle unfortunately made what you call fungible victims: the wife of Sergeant L, whom we [B, Silveria and I] killed because we considered him a torturer, went insane because she was
incapable of abstraction and had no orientation.

The cultural legacy of the armed struggle, of which you have spoken,
can also mean the ability to transform grief into something positive.

She – I would say not at all. Either we say that it was all terrorism
and speak about acts of folly, or we look at the origins of the phenomenon. From that point of view the situation has worsened. The cooper-
atives have to ask the Camorra who to employ. The recent case of
Enzo Fontana who was captured, they say, while he was trying to
commit a robbery, is emblematic of how the State talks one way and
acts another; it is useless to talk about the reintegration of prisoners if
they are then not allowed to reintegrate themselves, to develop fully
their capabilities and to maintain their families adequately. The temp-
tation to steal may then come, and at least one can understand it!

It was Senator Veca himself, a Communist, who vetoed Fontana's
request to go to work at the Fondazione Feltrinelli. The Communists
should have already made an examination of conscience over their history
a long time ago, before someone makes them do it.

Appendix 9: Bruno Laronga, 16 March 1990 – Questionnaire

1.
What were the family relationships in your original family? Do you have a favourable recollection of your family?

Good, with a natural mutual exchange of ideas, including those on our political choices.

Have you ever idealised one of your parents or a substitute for one of them?

It is not easy to idealise a parental figure. Perhaps you can idealise a person outside the family but close to it. Walter Alasia was the hero of my youth. Walter Alasia was a Communist combatant too. At San Severo [Foggia], where we lived before emigrating to the North, he belonged to the Communist Federation led by Secchia, one of the hardliners of the Communist Party. The comrades of that federation were eagerly waiting for the right moment, which they thought was very near. Following the attempt on Togliatti's life, the peasants occupied the town and did all kinds of riotous things. But the counter-order of the Communist Party made them feel like losers.

Did you ever have the feeling that you were deprived of something vital, of something very important in your childhood; that you were lacking something which it was your right to have?

Yes, stability. I have already mentioned that my family emigrated from San Severo to Sesto San Giovanni. In Sesto San Giovanni, in fact, all the defeated people of the South were reunited in a desire to do something different than they had done before or than their fathers had done.

Their common belonging to the Communist tradition was indeed an element of continuity. They left behind or lost everything except one thing when they emigrated, the feeling that everywhere there would be comrades with those same feelings and ideals that you had! This 'blood' tradition of the south married with the tradition of union struggle in the north and created a cultural landscape particularly favourable for armed struggle. My decision to join the armed struggle did not, however, come solely from this situation. I do not consider myself a child of the Italy of immigration.

I was an aristocrat who worked as a blue-collar worker [at Black & Decker] because in that way I could be a militant enrolled in the worker environment, in contact with the deepest needs of the workers. And when we blew up a director's car, the workers used to say that the next day it would be better to bring a machine-gun!

I would like to know how you felt about belonging to the armed struggle with regard to family dynamics. In opposition? (For example, the family did not want to discuss social problems or class struggle.)

Discreetly but clearly.

As a continuation? (The armed struggle manifests at society level what has already been experienced in a conflictual family situation.)

Absolutely untrue.

As an escape? (Better the armed struggle than the family.)

Out of the question: the armed struggle was like the greatest possible commitment. This concerns not just me. Militants often took as their *nom de guerre* the one their fathers as former partisans, like SS who chose to call himself Sirio. Siro also begins with 'S', like Spartacus. In a word, we felt a continuity with the Communist tradition.

**2.
Tell me about your reasons for joining the armed struggle. It is not really the political analysis that interests me, unless you want to go over it. I am curious above all to know what feelings led you to join the armed struggle: love of the cause? Dedication to a cause out of a deep conviction as to its rightness?**

A kind of inevitability about being involved to the hilt, a desire for lasting social justice.

A sense of your own greatness and/or of your own importance?

A little vanity plays a part in any big decision, all the more for people who are putting their lives at stake, even if only in a subjective sense.

3.
What was the occasion of your joining the armed struggle?

(a) Group friendships?

Yes, we were very much a troop.

(b) I was selected because I was already a sympathiser?

No.

(c) I still do not understand what brought it about?

No.

4.
What justified the killing of an enemy for you?

(a) It was necessary for the cause but I felt bad about it?

We did not hand out death light-heartedly; we very much felt our responsibility and the tragic quality of that action. Recognising another person as an enemy does, in any case, confer dignity upon him.

(b) He was an oppressor or a symbol of oppression or someone who worked zealously for those in power?

He was our opponent, the class enemy. He was a man who worked for those in power and worked hard. A personnel director, for example, cannot work for the good of others, as we do now, and as do many of our comrades on supervised parole or in work-release programmes; he has to pay attention only to the profit of the company.

Even so, the enemy was a man with his weaknesses and failings. Only a highly developed symbolism could have brought about a split like this.

(c) Nothing justified the killing of an enemy.

5.
What did the armed struggle mean principally for you?

(a) Annihilation of the oppressors?

(b) Creation of a more just society?

Yes.

6.
If the armed struggle was supposed to create a world founded on justice, did you consider yourselves as the direct artificers of this creation or its instruments?

Have you ever had the feeling that you could not have done otherwise?

It could not have been done differently. At least so it seemed. Artificers at the beginning, but then we discovered that we had brought on a practice, a level at such a height, that we ended up by being its instruments. The laws of war become absolute (armed conflict).

7.
Were there moments when you had doubts about the armed struggle or were you always in symbiosis with it?

Almost always in symbiosis. However, there were strong incentives for sticking doggedly with the original decision: the difficulties in returning to what was normal: an emotional extortion that was 'subjective' rather than objective, namely the prisoners from your own group.

8.
What was there about your militancy that most gratified you?

(a) A sense of defiance of society?

No. The fact of being totally at risk.

(b) Human relationships within the group?

That too.

(c) The interchangeability of roles? Both women and men can

**shoot and kill, both women and men can be heads of logistical
and operational networks.**

The same as in any other sector.

9.
**Did you ever feel tension between your femininity and belonging
to an armed group? Did the experience you had enrich you or
did you feel you had to give up a part of yourself? Having
listened to the interviews with women who were former
terrorists on 'La Notte della Repubblica', I got the impression
that there was a kind of hardening of the women comrades. Can
you confirm or deny this impression?**

**(a) Did devotion to the cause strengthen a man's love for his
own woman companion? Was he proud that his companion
fought alongside him?**

No, it was just a cause of further emotional tension and on the other
hand a life split in the manner of Dr Jekyll and Mr Hyde is unimagin-
able. You needed a companion with whom you could share the feelings and desires of such a tragic life. We spent a great deal of time
together, our whole militancy in Prima Linea, prison, dissociation. We
do not have the fragility of dreamers.

10.
What did distancing yourself from the armed struggle mean?

(a) Could you describe it as an emotional feeling?

That too.

(b) A rational decision?

That too.

(c) Moral uneasiness?

Principally because the damage seems irreparable so far, although some
big names are included among those who have pardoned us. Not, however, those of the relatives of dead persons who were not very promi-

nent. Those people would like us to pay a higher price than we are now paying.

11.
Why the cooperation with the justice system?

(*Unanswered.*)

12.
If you had to describe your former comrades' naming you as an accomplice, what would you call it?

(*Unanswered.*)

13.
How did you feel about the police who caught you and the judges who tried you?

(*Unanswered.*)

14.
Did the armed struggle leave behind any possibility of a cultural heritage or only a great deal of pain?

Pain, too, is a cultural heritage: from pain come great thoughts on man's make-up, on his strength and weakness in the world.

15.
What things do you now consider important in your life?

Stability, peace, an interest in those left behind, my children . . . some friends to exchange ideas with on all this.

16.
Is there anything about your life that you would like me to ask you about?

(*Unanswered.*)

Any questions of the interviewee for the interviewer?

No.

Appendix 10: Mario Ferrandi, 2 April 1990 – Questionnaire

1.
What were the family relationships in your original family?
Do you have a favourable recollection of your family?

Yes. My people never let me lack what was necessary. I was always at the centre of my mother's attention.

Did you ever idealise one of your parents or a substitute for one of them?

Yes, my partisan father.

Did you ever have the feeling that you were deprived of something vital, something very important, in your childhood, that you were lacking something which it was your right to have?

No.

I would like to know how you felt about belonging to the armed struggle with regard to family dynamics. In opposition? (For example, the family did not want to discuss social problems or class struggle?)

No.

As a continuation? (The armed struggle manifests at society level what has already been experienced in a conflictual family situation.)

No.

As an escape? (Better the armed struggle than the family.)

No.

2.
**Tell me about your reasons for joining Prima Linea. It is not
really a political analysis that interests me, unless you want to
go over it. I am curious above all to know what feelings led you
to join the armed struggle: enamourment of the cause?**
Dedication to a cause out of deep conviction as to its rightness?

The armed struggle was right for us because it let us expose the contradictions in social life, unmask the media that is even today still in
subjugation. In any event our elective father, the Communist Party,
had educated us in a double morality. And then we did worse than
those whom we intended to fight.

A sense of your own greatness and/or of your own importance?

For many comrades, yes. Indeed I was living as though I were a hero.
Everyone came to be accepted the way they were, handsome or ugly,
and to feel themselves important and influential in resolving the adolescent problems they found themselves involved in. And together with
the adolescent problems they also resolved social problems. They changed
their names, and that was cathartic.

Our *noms de guerre*, though, were wholly random ones, that is, they
did not have reference to personages in the Communist tradition.
Barbone's was 'Ernesto' and the reference was obviously to 'Che'.

3.
What was the occasion of your joining the armed struggle?

(a) Group friendships?

In any case the friendships I sought.

(b) I was selected because I was already a sympathiser?

(c) I still do not understand what brought it about?

4.
What justified the killing of an enemy for you?

(a) It was necessary for the cause but I felt bad about it?

(b) He was an oppressor or a symbol of oppression or one who worked zealously for those in power?

For us it was justifiable to kill when a grave wrong cried out for vengeance. I killed one drug dealer and I was not sorry about it, just as it did not trouble the Carabinieri at the time. In any event Continuous Struggle was responsible for the first political murder with the Calabresi crime. At that time there was a committee against State massacres that the Red Brigades, Dario Fo, Feltrinelli and Sofri belonged to. Speaking of Sofri, he may not have given the order to kill Calabresi himself, but that crime in any case grew out of that environment. Vigilantism is primordial vengeance, an animal rather than a war reaction.

(c) Nothing justified the killing of an enemy.

5.
What, above all, did the armed struggle mean for you?

(a) Annihilation of the oppressors?

(b) Creation of a more just society?

For us who were in the avant-garde, yes. We wanted to create a more just society where no one would be marginalised, that is, unable to develop fully his or her creative potential. The majority of the movement were just anti-authoritarian.

6.
If the armed struggle was supposed to create a world founded on justice, did you consider yourselves the direct artificers of this creation or its instruments?

Have you ever had the feeling that you could not have done otherwise?

Personally, no. I would say that we were living in dualistic terms: a little interpreting the needs of the 'movement' and of the 'class', and a little striving toward the realisation of these needs. And then there were those who strove too hard. At any rate that permitted endless discussions about subjectivity.

7.
Were there moments when you had doubts about the armed struggle or were you always in symbiosis with it?

When three of my friends who were drunk in a bar killed people who tried to throw them out. The killing was then justified as vigilantism against the oppressors of the proletariat. For me this was an ethical watershed. I should have denounced them to the direction. Instead, partly because of the uselessness of the thing, I went to England. In England I experienced the English prisons, which at the least are tougher than ours, but the prison guards are trained to respect the prisoners, any prisoner. In England the police go around unarmed, because it is inconceivable that a robber would shoot. Civic education has had an influence even on the behaviour of criminals.

8.
What was there about your militancy that most gratified you?

(a) A sense of defiance of society?

To have an impact on the life of society. To exercise real power. The pleasure of exercising a real counter-power: we blew up the rails of the Metro because we wanted to participate in the festivities of the Ascension. In any case no military ethic was formulated. We demanded to be treated as political prisoners, but we never respected the Geneva Convention.

(b) Human relations within the group?

(c) Interchangeability of roles? Both women and men can shoot and kill, both women and men can be heads of logistical and operational networks.

9.
Have you ever felt a tension between your femininity and belonging to an armed group? Did the experience you had enrich you or did you feel that you had to give up a part of yourself? Having listened to the interviews with women who were former terrorists on 'Notte della repubblica', I got the impression there was a kind of hardening of the women comrades. Can you confirm or deny this impression?

(a) Did devotion to the cause strengthen a man's love for his woman companion? Was he proud that his companion fought alongside him?

Mara and I met at the Tobagi trial.

10.
What did distancing yourself from the armed struggle mean?

(a) Could you describe it as an emotional feeling?

(b) Was it a rational decision? (I want to survive, now that it is all over and make plans for the future.)

For me penitentism was an instrument of struggle that was not just against us. I support it because it is producing a tremendous cultural revulsion.

And then the cultural machine runs by itself. To justify penitentism it would be necessary to change the whole system. Then a criminal background would no longer exist and I could be reinstated as a normal citizen.

(c) Moral uneasiness?

Yes, of course. Now we can see that there is no Communist ethic, but only a human ethic.

(d) Desperation?

Yes, desperation comes too when we see that we have been fooled through our own fault, that we fell right into the trap that the P2 and other powerful economic interests, of which the State constitutes a business committee, prepared for us. Once we fell into that trap, we got ever more entangled through our double Communist ethic in a tunnel without any exit.

11.
Why the cooperation with the justice system?

So that I could feel myself to be just a citizen without anyone calling me a traitor and a villain.

12.
If you had to describe your former comrades' naming you as an accomplice, what would you call it?

People who put us in the stocks, that the Parliament prepared for us. But penitentism set off a chain reaction that for the judges was not supposed ever to stop until the arrest of the last of the fugitives.

13.
How did you feel about the police who arrested you and the judges who tried you?

Some judges, behind the mask, are very humane and respectful of a man. But then you meet careerists who use crooked methods to get around you and they are disgusting.
    There are those who try to understand.

14.
Did armed struggle leave behind any possibility of a cultural heritage or just a great deal of pain?

A cultural heritage of unanswered questions: the one on a democratic maturity that does not exist. The judges cannot take our cooperation for granted. In the future they will have to be careful about favouring penitentism because they are destroying people; it might be a good idea for them to use consultants.
    And then there is a whole way of life and a press that makes light of marginalisation.

15.
What things do you now consider important in your life?

To initiate a cultural movement that would transform the values one normally believes in: honour and faithfulness.

16.
Is there anything in your life that you would like me to ask you about?

(*Unanswered.*)

Any questions of the interviewee for the interviewer?

Barbone told me in prison that the problem of terrorism is a problem of those who lose relative to those who win. If we had won, there would not have been any terrorism. What do you think?

Appendix 11: Vincenza Fioroni – Questionnaire

1.
What were the relationships in your original family? Do you have a favourable recollection of your family?

A relationship that I would say was normal. We were always close to one another with a good deal of affection and we helped one another. I saw my parents very often and my two small daughters stayed with them frequently. I was separated and my family always helped me and they knew nothing about my participation in the armed struggle.

Have you ever idealised one of your parents or a substitute for one of them?

No.

Did you ever have the feeling that you were deprived of something vital, of something very important, that you were lacking something which it was your right to have?

Starting with adolescence I felt deprived of my own locality; I had emigrated as a child and up until around 20 years of age I was home-sick for my place even though I appreciated the prosperity and culture acquired in a big city.

I would like to know how you felt about belonging to the armed struggle with regard to family dynamics. In opposition? (For example, the family did not want to discuss social problems or class struggle.)

My family was not aware of my political choices; the affection I had for them made me want to avoid conflicts with them and the girls were too young to have anything in common with me.

As a continuation? (The armed struggle manifests at society level what has already been experienced in a conflictual family situation.)

As an escape? (Better the armed struggle than the family.)

2.
Tell me about your reasons for joining Prima Linea. It is not really a political analysis that interests me, unless you want to go over it. I am curious above all to know what feelings led you to join the armed struggle: love of the cause?

Yes, certainly. For 10 years I had been engaged in social struggles in unions, in school and in my neighbourhood. It seemed to me that nothing had changed and so the armed struggle was the last resort.

Dedication to a cause out of deep conviction as to its rightness?

I do not know whether it was exactly the rightness of the revolution, but the rightness of my personal commitment, yes.

A sense of your own greatness and/or of your own importance?

No.

3.
What was the occasion of your joining the armed struggle?

(a) Group friendships?

Several people I had known for some time who unbeknown to me belonged to Prima Linea and who knew me as a person always involved in struggles in the city, began to talk to me about Prima Linea to the point of my practically joining after my disappointment with the earlier failed struggles. I went into Prima Linea at the beginning of the eighties; although there had been an armed struggle for years, I had not wanted to be involved and so I joined Prima Linea when it was already in crisis and for me it was really the last resort; after years of refusing to join violent organisations, I thought that perhaps there were no other avenues open. In 1980 I was no longer young, but I was certainly in a crisis over the political practices I had experienced up to that time, a crisis that did not end when I joined Prima Linea, but rather, after a little 'internal' knowledge of it – my active membership lasted 5 months – deepened to the point I decided to dissociate.

(b) I was selected because I was already a sympathiser.

(c) I still do not understand what brought it about.

4.
What justified the killing of an enemy for you?

(a) It was necessary for the cause but I felt bad about it.

(b) He was an oppressor or a symbol of oppression or one who worked zealously for those in power?

First of all it must be remembered that the friend/enemy dichotomy was not invented by us; rather, perhaps we took this dichotomy literally and if one has an 'enemy', history teaches that it is necessary to eliminate him. We were the direct heirs of the concept that there are just and unjust wars; we had chosen our activities as the situation demanded as a just manifestation, as a just occupation and, hence, as a just war. Our concern, not just that of the bands but what was internal to the entire movement, was not with persons, with men, with a concept of life and death, but with institutions; and so we were not concerned with the elimination of a person but of what he represented. Fortunately I never had to decide about the death of a person, much less materially to follow through on it.

(c) Nothing justified the killing of an enemy.

5.
What, above all, did the armed struggle mean for you?

(a) Annihilation of the oppressors?

(b) Creation of a more just society?

Yes, even though I did not have a clear idea of that future society. A model to imitate did not exist even among the socialist societies, because the desire for justice and liberty was broader, deeper and more radical than what could be realised in the form of a totalitarian state.

6.
If the armed struggle was supposed to create a world founded on justice, did you consider yourselves the direct artificers of this creation or its instruments? Did you ever have the feeling that it could not have been done differently?

The idea and the value of being leaders, in the sense of participating in changes as more than a delegate, was certainly strong in me. I never considered myself an instrument but always a person entirely involved.

7.
Were there moments when you had doubts about the armed struggle or were you always in symbiosis with it?

Never really in symbiosis, given the brief experience.

8.
What was there about your militancy that most gratified you?

(a) A sense of defiance of society?

No.

(b) Human relations within the group?

Yes and the feeling of being yourself.

(c) Interchangeability of roles? Both women and men can shoot and kill, both women and men can be heads of logistical and operational networks.

When I joined the armed struggle I had already won a feeling of equality with men as regards rights and duties and I didn't have to fight any battles for recognition.

The fact that in Prima Linea roles were distributed on the basis of capabilities and did not depend on sex was not surprising.

9.

Did you ever feel tension between your femininity and belonging to an armed group? Did the experience you had enrich you or did you feel that you had to give up a part of yourself? Having listened to interviews with women who were former terrorists on 'La Notte della Repubblica', I got the impression there was a kind of hardness in the women comrades. Can you confirm or deny this impression?

I did not perceive any hardness. It seemed to me rather that every woman recounted her own story and so, inevitably and fortunately, differences emerged.

(a) Did dedication to the cause strengthen a man's love for his woman companion? Was he proud that his companion fought alongside him?

10.

What did distancing yourself from the armed conflict mean?

(a) Could you describe it as an emotional feeling?

(b) A rational decision? (I want to survive, now that it is all over and make plans for the future.)

A feeling of maturity, an awareness, a desire to know reality through readings that are not schematic. However, the others also ought to read reality without preconceived ideas, among which one of the most dangerous is that of 'enemy'. A good many persons have not gotten over that idea with regard to us.

(c) Moral uneasiness?

Partly because taking stock of one's own mistakes creates moral uneasiness, but also a great deal of determination to learn how to be
more careful and not to make mistakes any more.

(d) Desperation?

No, just a great desire to build positively.

11.
Why the cooperation with the justice system?

Absolutely necessary to put an end to ideological deviations. If there
were a culture of cooperation instead of a culture of silence in relation
to organised crime, the Mafia and Camorra would not have any ground
to operate on.

12.
**If you had to describe your former comrades' naming you as an
accomplice, what would you call it?**

Hard choices but right ones, especially with hindsight.

13.
**How did you feel about the police who caught you and the
judges who tried you?**

Gratitude and respect.

14.
**Did the armed struggle leave behind any possibility of a cultural
heritage or just a great deal of pain?**

Pain certainly, but also a subjective cultural heritage. If this culture
becomes a collective and dialectical encounter, a basis can be created
for not repeating the mistakes.

15.
What things do you now consider important in your life?

Thinking, a search for values, rebuilding relations with my children, work, reintegration into society.

16.
Is there anything in your life that you would like me to ask you about?

(*Unanswered.*)

Any questions of the interviewee for the interviewer?

No.

Appendix 12: Meeting with Vincenza Fioroni, 30 May 1990

Vincenza Fioroni is 40 years old and has beautiful, long blonde hair and a well groomed though unostentations appearance.

Dissociated, her legal status is that of a person on supervised probation; she must go daily to sign a required form and notify police headquarters if she leaves Bergamo. The prosecution for the Galli murder (1980) has not yet been completed. In the lower court she was given 9 years for material complicity in the murder along with participation in a robbery in which she had acted as a lookout. Fabrizio Giai named her as an accomplice.

She was instead found not guilty of the Fara attempted murder (1980) for lack of proof. For this attempted murder she was named as an accomplice by Viscardi.

Vincenza Fioroni is obviously in anguish over the possibility that the sentence may increase to 16 years in the new trial. 'You see, if I go back inside, this ceramics workshop, where people are working who were willing to take a chance with me, could not keep going. I am very proud of my workshop and I would be sorry to lose it. And I am also hoping to involve it in helping save drug addicts.

That is really a great idea. There is a great need for initiatives of this kind. And it is not completely without risk. While drug

addicts may behave well, they can also take advantage.

If everything ends well with the trial, that is certainly not a danger that frightens me. But I am afraid that everything is not going to end well in the trial.

F told the truth regarding my participation in the Galli murder, that my house was available but was not programmed as a refuge in the Galli murder. It just happened that a traffic accident (running into a squad car of the Carabinieri) forced the actual perpetrators of the murder to seek refuge in my house. I felt that I had been gotten around. Because if they had asked for the house as an escape refuge, I would have given it to them. But in fact I did not know anything.

When I heard of the murder I thought it was the Red Brigades.

You were saying that A exculpated you. . . .

Yes, but since he subsequently retracted, it was not completely believed. Bruno Laronga and Silveria Russo also tried to exculpate me and I am very grateful to them for that. . . .

Your militancy was very brief but it fell right in the bloodiest period of Prima Linea.

I told you that at that time I would have given my house as a refuge for the fugitives. But I did not do what they accused me of. And then, look, Prima Linea was in a deep crisis. The new members wanted more discussion at a time when it was decreasing between the operative units and the new members because it was not approved of by the National Command.

The Vaccher, Paoletti and Galli murders were decided by the National Command. In any case I was assigned to work with the masses in the sense of having Prima Linea put down roots in the neighbourhood. My past union activity at school made me particularly suitable in their eyes for carrying on that work.

But as far as you are concerned, why did you decide to become active in Prima Linea?

I think that for me it was a last resort after having seen first hand our total impotence to change things without violence. I was an elementary school teacher.

I had accepted a handicapped little girl in my class (1975/1976) and the director did not like it. I brought sex education books into class and the director did not like it. Then both the director and I got transferred.

Following the massacre of Piazza Fontana, we were rebuked by the director of the school, where we were only in training, because they had seen us on television protesting the Fascist massacre. At the time of the Moro kidnapping and the killing of his escort, we were rebuked by our union because we had not left our jobs to go and demonstrate against this zillionth act of terrorism.

But I had penal and civil responsibility for the children in my class. In a word, whatever we did was wrong. Meanwhile anger and frustration grew within me. You can be sure that many did not jump into the armed struggle not because they were convinced that it was wrong, but because of personal obstacles. And then the group was very democratic because roles were determined on the basis of a person's capabilities and not on the basis of sex.

Your political programme too, if I am not mistaken, was intended to be democratic in the sense of aiming at the establishment of a more just, more egalitarian, society. The dictatorship of the proletariat instead was in the plans of the Red Brigades.

Yes. There was no intention of establishing a totalitarian state. In reality, anyway, I did not want to establish anything. It was more than anything else a rebellious feeling, and we thought that the rebellion would never end, that it would last all our lives.

Well, I understand rebellion, and struggle too, but honest ones. An opponent has to have a chance to defend himself. But the murder of one who has his back to you is absolutely repugnant; that is like a leopard who attacks you in the back, not a combatant.

Yes, but the war was a just one, and so that murder too was legitimate or at least for us it was. After all, Galli, who had amended the penal law to make accomplices of those who had performed only logistical support functions without perhaps knowing what they were going to do at that particular moment, lived like an enemy who gave a person no possibility of defending himself.

How did your children take your militancy and your arrest?

There has always been affection and it is only now that we are beginning to deal with certain subjects.

After my arrest they chose the path of silence.

The older one has succeeded in dealing with her suffering: she told
me once that she is more mature than others. I feel guilty for having
given them an insecure adolescence.

I instead had a humiliating adolescence. I left Umbria and for 3
years in middle school my teachers called me a hillbilly, but a smart
one.

I was ashamed to say that I helped my mother work as a domestic
help because I thought I would be made even more the butt of jokes.
I am divorced now and my children were entrusted to my husband
when I was arrested. I was fortunate enough to have a sister who always
brought them to visit me, perhaps by making up imaginary excuses.

**If you do not mind, I would like to hear about the trial and
prison. How did you women dress, how did you act?**

When we had to appear in court we tried to have a little colour in our
faces and to be well-groomed because we seemed to reek of prison
and instead we wanted to seem normal. Primarily we wanted to save
ourselves.

When our relatives brought us some pretty clothes, we took turns
wearing them; one day I would wear something, the day after, someone else. But we felt that during the trial the women jurors judged our
way of dressing too. I went through the whole Galli trial wearing a
grey dress.

**The stereotype of a woman is perpetuated by women themselves.
A woman, being much more narcissistic than a man, attaches
much more importance to physical appearance and hence is
punished in this too. She no longer has any right to this narcissism
now that she is considered guilty even before being found guilty.
Have they the presumption to see a woman's guilt even by her
dress, while for a man this presumption does not exist?**

Anyway at the trial they made me look like a crafty person. They
thought that I was such an important person that I could make leaders
of the calibre of Silveria Russo and Bruno Laronga defend me. In

reality they did it of their own accord. It was a decision or better, in this case, an emotion, which was entirely personal, just as their path to dissociation is a very personal one.

You spoke about the women on the jury. What can you tell me about the women prison guards? I know that there was a victim among the women prison guards in Turin. Was she crippled by a female command of Prima Linea?

Women prison guards impose their authority purely by force. Just imagine, they need to have only a fifth grade education to handle a job that ought to involve rehabilitating the prisoner!

And then it is surprising that some women too know how to rub it in and enjoy doing it. I have had an awful time with the women guards. In Latina, Fulvia Maglietta was absolutely hysterical. She wanted to know her comrades' opinion of her behaviour, that is, of her having fallen in love with the DIGOS [Division of General Investigations of the National Police] agent who caught her. Also there was SB of the Red Brigades. I really feared for her life. I asked the guards to let me speak to the director, but they told me scornfully that the director was not at my disposal.

In the end I had to threaten her to keep her from leaving the cell; I myself deliberately said things to her that could have been misinterpreted as death threats. It happened another time that we of Prima Linea kept watch during our hour out in the air to prevent attacks against the penitents. In the end I got the reputation of being the least trustworthy comrade, and then I asked the director to stop my transfer to Voghera, where all the obdurate subversives were to be channelled.

Fortunately I avoided Voghera.

We may say that this time you used a death image, communicated as a threat to Fulvia Maglietta, in order to protect life and you succeeded in your intention to protect her safety by keeping this threat always at a symbolic level.

You are right and it is a thing that pleases me very much to help build an atmosphere of reconciliation. I would like to be more active in this field, perhaps helping the magistrates by using the wealth of experience I acquired in the armed struggle. But the only help they want is that of the co-defendants and from me they want it least of all because they consider me a sneak.

It seems to me that this contrast between the esteem you have for the magistrates, at least for those you have known and their way of thinking about you, is a thing that is more troublesome and painful than even the idea of ending up in jail again.

Yes, unfortunately....

That is normal enough. You do not get a chance to demonstrate your healing impulses. You cannot use them. With the danger that they may get directed toward erroneous objects or get their aim transmuted.... An atmosphere of reconciliation can create a new society, as the armed struggle certainly could not. I see that you like very much to create; your ceramic pieces show that.

Before making articles I did sculptures, all with empty bellies that remind me of the ditches I used to play in when I was a child in Umbria.

During my whole time in prison I dreamed of Umbria because my serenity is in the earth. It may also be that the empty bellies are a visualisation of my sense of guilt for having brought so much suffering upon my daughters.

Appendix 13: Joint Meeting with Silveria Russo and Bruno Laronga, 3 August 1990

This third meeting with Silveria Russo and Bruno Laronga was requested by the interviewees themselves.

The questions they were asked derive from comments of criticism or agreement that Silveria Russo and Bruno Laronga made relative to the research methods (too psychological and too little historical–sociological) and its contents (their position relative to the penitents is said not to have been clarified as much as it should have been).

Three questions were prepared (those preceded by numbering) with the intention of testing more the cognitive than the psychological aspect of their meaning. The others emerged from the conversation based on the ideas discussed in the paragraph on the psychological instruments of interpretation.

1.
**We have, alongside the lucidity of a plan which requests a
historical–critical focus in order to be understood, an appeal to
schizophrenia, which cannot be understood by a historical–
critical focus. How do you explain this combination of the
rational (counter-power against a power that excludes) and the
irrational (split between feeling and reason), which is not
brought about by illness?**

Bruno – If the lucidity of the 'plan' was badly explained, the appeal
to schizophrenia was explained even worse.

The latter is produced by defence mechanisms of memory and by a
desire for removal when dealing with the problem of living with a
burdensome past that is as difficult to justify as it is to bear. On the
other hand, being motivated by a positive Utopia (a desire for social
justice and a world of free and equal persons, where the seizure of
power by the proletariat represented only a step toward this liberation. . . .) and exercising a murderous practice (even though they are
things that are very, very impossible to mix) produced a kind of split
that only our ideology was able, for a very brief period, to put together.

So the problem is to understand how an ideology, extreme as you
wish, was able to bring about this joining together. Out of what suggestions, happenings, expectations did an extremist sector of the left
make the decision that it was the moment to take up arms:

(a) 'The war could have become a prolongation of politics by spe-
    cific means' when even death seemed to become a variable of
    engaging in politics (massacres, deaths in the public square, the
    reorganisation of fascist-like organisations, etc.).

(b) The myth of Che Guevara, the war of liberation in Cuba, the birth
    of armed groups in Europe, the revival of the IRA and the Pales-
    tinians on the one side and, on the other, the coup against a de-
    mocracy in Chile, completed the framework of a democracy blocked
    and subject to coup attempts (1974–5).

(c) The powerlessness of the union tradition to resolve the social conflict
    and the attempt to give a stable organisation to the sporadic use
    of 'force' by sectors of the working class (for example, picketing,
    goons, inside demonstrations, flying squads in industrial zones against
    strike breakers).

This mix of elements, partly defensive, partly offensive, could have given a semblance of legitimacy to the recourse to weapons: it should not be forgotten that the majority of the armed actions had a 'propaganda' character and some had a 'Robin Hood' aspect: the kidnapping of a butcher to drive down the price of meat in working-class areas, the theft and free distribution of ATM tickets... all the actions that had a 'romantic' flavour but at the same time a most practical and fruitful result: proletarians have always and everywhere co-existed with illegality and violence.

An entirely different thing is the abstractness of pure politics: what part did the workers play in the Moro kidnapping and all the others? What did they know about the absolute 'enmity' of judges like Alessandrini and Galli?

This level of practice overrode everything even then and we were perfectly aware of it. In the end, we lost the original rationale for the actions, and just the action remained: the laws of war have taken the place of the laws of politics and that led first to complete isolation and then to utter defeat.

Silveria – To begin with, it would be necessary to discuss the 'lucidity of the plan'. The plan was in reality a Utopia of a better society (Communist?) but in my opinion without knowing what this could possibly be. Certainly it was not real socialism, the effects of which were visible to everyone. But in the end what was this Communism, leaving aside reference to the classics (ownership of the means of production as a goal; a period of a dualism of power as a passage to it)?

So, it may be said that 'a great many were generically in favour of a more just world', one without exploitation. But why could this not have been the realisation of a Gospel Utopia? Many of us were in fact Catholics who had distanced ourselves precisely because the Church, as it was, did not respond to the demands of 'integral humanism'.

I would say that first of all it would be necessary to reduce the premise and in this way the second point in question would also be reduced. That it was concretely a matter of schizophrenic behaviour is beyond doubt (that is, a split between sentiments and reason): it started from a solidaristic zeal, one that was Utopian (the kingdom of God on earth or a society of producers, there is little difference) and it ended with outcomes that negate, in effect, man and his right to life, leaving aside a more just life, an end perhaps forced by circumstances, but the result does not change.

I have thought many times that 'it was fortunate that they arrested me', because what kind of society would it have been, one that was created from a victory of this kind of behaviour? A monster. Or perhaps – second scenario – the very ones who had fought for years might, at the moment of victory, have dissociated themselves, as did Guevara.

So I would say that the simultaneous presence of reason and antireason was there from the beginning in the desire to create a Utopia (peaceful and communitarian), but also in believing that only violence is the 'yeast of history' (and this is an exact ideological reference). Hence, for those who were Catholic, in thinking that the eschatological Utopia could be realised only in symbiosis with other beliefs (in a way, that the Church was rotten in our eyes was just an excuse for giving credence to our option for 'integral poverty', which was, of course, a political view in any case). And it was right there, in a choice that was of course ideological, that there was the cancer of a split, in the plan as in the persons who implemented it. In the end, I would answer that the split was not between the plan (lucid, noble) and the reality of the men who have to implement it, but between the reality, because it comes first, and the plan.

It is an error inherent in an ideology or in an ideological vision of the world: what is, what ought to be . . . party/class . . . state/civil society . . . where does it lead to historically? And where is man in it?

Bruno – With regard to what ought to be, I get the impression that we have passed from one thing that ought to be to another. And even now, anyway, if we wanted to be perfectly consistent, we would insist on a radical choice, because the most authentic example of a faith that ought to be is the monk who gives up life in society.

Silveria – That is not necessary at all. There is a middle way between ideology, as a literal application of idealisation and a levelling that lacks values. There is a possibility of staying within a reality that begins with moral values, without, however, making them absolute, but rather renewing them and vivifying them in relation to others. That is what a certain ecclesiastical reality seeks, but it is also what, today in general, understanding history is, as a continual renewal, as rupture, as the rethinking of ideologies understood as a crystallisation of what exists.

2.
Was not the fact of your negating the needs of certain persons inconsistent with seeing life as worthy of being lived only if it is oriented toward the needs of others?

Bruno – Among all the difficulties that recourse to arms entailed, this one was the hardest to overcome: it is truer to say that it was never overcome. However, it is certain that clandestinity, living a double existence made up of sacrifices, is, in a way, ascetical and pure (we changed names, we lived on the minimum necessary and the personal was completely sacrificed to the political) and gave us an impression that our lives too could be sacrificed in order to reach an ideal; a high price for any ideal, but this seemed to be the price the situation required: but we did not in any event reach the point of being as indifferent to life and death as the hero in *For Whom the Bell Tolls*, who goes away whistling after the death of his woman companion in battle. It was a life so oriented towards a presumed sacrifice-for-others as to include the sacrifice of some and of course of oneself. Ideology short-circuits conscience and guilt, for which reason one ends up attributing to the 'enemy' a universal knowledge of one's own place within the adversary's camp. It is a speculative character that makes it possible to make this leap: on the one hand we demand of ourselves as avant-garde of the class a maximum of political awareness and on the other we attribute it to the 'class enemy', while often on either side of the barricades only a partial or provisional political awareness is possessed. In any case it was expected that each would draw the consequences of his or her position, subjective or objective as the case might be, given that a war had been declared, even if by a tiny minority.

You were a chief. What was the relationship between a chief and those who received orders from a chief or, let us say, suggestions, given that Prima Linea was not a hierarchical organisation like the Red Brigades?

Bruno – I liked to be with everybody, everybody in war uniform, I mean. But whether they were persons who were exceptionally capable or were scamps was of little interest to me. S was much more the kind of hero who surrounds himself with henchmen who are ready to do his bidding.

Silveria – Bruno is more like an anti-hero.

Or perhaps we might say that you lived like a hero and not like a military chief. The hero can understand the weakness of others and try to compensate for it with his own greater willingness to take risks; he can establish a relationship between equals with the men he fights alongside of. A military chief is more oriented toward the efficiency of military service and less likely to understand the weaknesses of others. For him human errors tend to be identified as mistakes involving lack of will.

Silveria – There is truth in that, Bruno.

With regard to your question, I think I have already answered the first point. There was indeed an enormous inconsistency.

3.
Political criminality and common crime. You do not have anything to do with this second kind of crime. But then there should not have been any instrumental relationships with common criminals. They denounce the Christian Democratic Party for relations with the Mafia and the Camorra. I do not see why they should not denounce you too. What were your relations in prison with common criminals?

Bruno – We have never had anything to do with common crime if by this term you mean the big cartels of the Mafia and Camorra kind; nor have they ever wanted to have anything to do with us, given that they are the other face of power, not the abstract and universal one, but the very material and horrible one that we have here and now. With thieves, robbers and outlaws of every kind and species there is an objective connection: they were the proletarians of the working-class districts who lived in the factories and the streets that we frequented; this meant that in some way we had to concern ourselves in prison with their difficulties; with their relations with the magistrates, the lawyers and the guards, and here and there we tried to limit the arrogance of the strong toward the weak, since the prison environment is the height of violence.

Objective relationships are obligatory when one shares the same conditions, in the same place, for years; you get to the point of having the same attitudes toward the guards, the food, the common areas; it is inevitable (there remain enormous differences in the use of free time and solitude: TV/books, study/pastimes, hierarchy/democracy, etc.).

The difference with the Christian Democrats is the fact that they do not share our fate: in my opinion they are to a certain extent right. I do not in fact find that the jails are full of Mafia people and corrupt Christian Democrats! The Christian Democrats are politicians in the strong traditional meaning of the word and they keep the use of force well away from themselves and have recourse to it at a distance, without – if possible – leaving a trace. We presumed to unite these functions in a military–political way, in the single framework of the militant organisation; with us the one who made the decision and the one who carried it out was very often the same person.

Silveria – I am concerned as far as it regards my doing what was proper and nothing more. But I have to say that I have never liked 'common' criminals, nor have I ever agreed to become 'proletarianised' in prison, which was typical of brigade members (but it was an instrumental manoeuvre). I did not accept their culture or their way of acting, partly because in prison there was an atmosphere of domination and of patronage for the most part. There was indeed encounter, perhaps with someone who wanted to be different or who was in a crisis and those who were in crisis were generally the drug addicts, because those who belonged to a gang thought only about getting out of prison as soon as possible and without risking anything. Then, outside, they begin again. We, so long as we were not really crushed, were never opportunistic with the authorities. . . .

The 'common' criminals never liked us, neither when we engaged in struggles (because we broke the balance of power created within the prison, which for them meant being able to traffic in tranquillity and without controls), nor when we dissociated (because the prison was no longer a free zone, a glass bell). If anything, it was the Ministry that for organisational reasons of its own induced us at a certain point to adopt the idea of an 'undifferentiated' penal treatment. But if the common criminals bring drugs or other things inside clandestinely? Everybody is silent, because all are subject to the same penal treatment.

And of course there were some among us who supported this idea with a populist logic that I find old-fashioned.

Let us now come to the penitents. Would you define your position better. . . .

Bruno – The first comment is that they let their personal destinies prevail over those of the group: very few thought of their personal decision in political terms and even fewer were concerned about it in social terms, even among themselves. It is certain that if they had waited for a year or so they would have dissociated together with the majority, but it was certainly difficult to foresee all this at the time of the arrest. Some of us never thought that decision was justified because they thought they were pretty strong and did not understand weakness, even the very human weakness that fear induces; fear of arrest, of long years in prison and the very harsh conditions for the 'specials'; there were some who went crazy in those conditions and never recovered, some died . . . so this is no exaggeration. In any case I think that many of the penitents were individuals who were more or less consciously forced by us to do things the weight and the discipline (interior and other) of which they could not bear; so a large part of the errors was in our appraisement of persons, the more so the more responsible we were. This meant that in Prima Linea (with some tragic exceptions) a prudent judgement always prevailed that the power of life and death was not to be exercised within the organisation: in the event of infractions, even very serious ones, people were only removed from the organisation, with the risk of having someone in circulation who knew a great deal, but accepting it. It fell to me to have to judge the behaviour of some persons who were thought to have something treasonous about them; I never issued death-sentence judgements. Our relationship with penitents in prison was that of forcing ourselves to understand what had happened. They often fell into an irremediable state of separation, for which reason it seems that they had always and solely to excuse themselves, when they did not deny their decision. They bear a burden heavier than ours and I think they find themselves very badly off in this condition; I could not stand being in the company of many of them precisely for that reason, even though, in an attempt to think my past right, I have gone down this entire road time and again. In the end it must be understood that often it is not the political people who influenced the common criminals, but the reverse: in the prison universe the penitents are despicable and the worst thing you can think of. Some have interiorised this conception of penitentism by substituting for it the misery of their condition in prison (it is well to remember that they live in prison always very isolated and in complete paranoia: like those who have their food tasted before they eat it).

Silveria – I suggest that you give some thought to the fact or perhaps insert it in the last part of your research, that utilising the law on penitents perhaps served many comrades by their not having a need to think.

It was through continually deeper thinking that we obtained reductions in our sentences as dissociated persons.

Why, in your opinion, were there more dissociated persons in Prima Linea and more penitents and obdurate persons in the Red Brigades?

Bruno – Because for us the collectivity had much more importance than it did in the Red Brigades. We dissociated *en masse*. We became a problem for the judiciary.

References

Adler, F. (1977), 'The Interaction between Women's Emancipation and Female Criminality: a Cross-cultural Perspective', *International Journal of Criminology and Penology*, **5**, p. 101.

Alali, A. O. and Eke, K. K. (eds) (1991), *Media Coverage of Terrorism* (Sage).

Ambroset, S. (1984), *Criminologia femminile* (Milan: Unicopli).

Barash, D. (1980), *Sociobiologia e comportamento* (Milan: Franco Angeli).

Barthes, R. (1963), *Essais critiques* (Paris: Editions du Seuil).

Barthes, R. (1977), *Fragments d'un discours amoureux* (Paris: Editions du Seuil).

Barnhurst, K. G. (1991), 'The Literature of Terrorism', in Alali and Eke, *Media Coverage*.

Bassiouni, M. C. (1987), *Legal Responses to International Terrorism* (Boston, Mass.: Martinus Nijhoof).

Bertrand, M. A. (1969), 'Self-image and Delinquency: a Contribution to the Study of Female Criminality and Women's Image', *Acta Criminologica*, January.

Bishop, C. (1931), *Women and Crime* (London: Chatto & Windus).

Blankenburg, E., Reifner, U. and Gorges, I. (1982), *Rechtsberatung: Soziale Definition von Rechtsproblemen durch Rechtsberatungsangebote* (Darmstadt/Neuwied: Luchterhand).

Bossle, L. (1978), 'Soziologie und Psycholgie des Radikalismus Phaenomens in der Politik', in *Extremismus im demokratischen Rechtsstaat*, ed. M. Funk (Dusseldorf: Droste) p. 64.

Brock-Utne, B. (1989), *La Pace donna* (Turin: Edizioni Gruppo Abele). (Original title: *Educating for Peace: A Feminist Perspective.*)

Brunetta, G. (1985), *Studi di Aggiornamento Sociale* (Milan: Edizioni Progetto Scuola).

Calvi, M. (ed.) (1982), *Estremismo politico* (Milan: Franco Angeli) pp. 122–33.

Cesa-Bianchi, M., (1987), 'Definizione, Indirizzi Metodi Della Psicologia', in Gulotta, G. (ed.), *Trattato di Psicologia Giudiziaria* (Milan: Giuffrè).

Chomsky, N. (1986), *Pirates & Emperors: International Terrorism in the Real World* (Brattleboro, VT: Amana).

Cowie, J., Cowie, V., and Slater, E. (1968), *Delinquency in Girls* (London: Heinemann).

Crespi, F. (1978), *Esistenza e simbolico: Prospective per una cultura alternativa* (Milan: Feltrinelli).

de Beauvoir, S. (1949), *Le dexième sexe* (Paris: Gallimard).

de Cataldo Neuburger, L. (1987), 'The Death Penalty', *Revue Internationale de Droit Penale, 3°et 4° trimestres 1987*, pp. 699–719.

de Cataldo Neuburger, L. (1988), *Psicologia della testimonianza e prova testimoniale* (Milan: Giuffrè).

de Cataldo Neuburger, L. (1992), 'Arrivare ad una decisione', in L. de Cataldo

Neuburger (ed.), *Chiamata in correità e psicologia del pentitismo* (Padua: Cedam) pp. 185–223.

Di Carmelo, G., (ed) (1989), *Eravamo terroristi: lettere dal carcere* (Milan: Edizioni Paoline).

Der Spiegel (1977), 'Die Terroristinnen', 8 August.

Der Spiegel (1981), 'Wir Fuehlten Uns Einfach Staerker', 11 May.

Der Spiegel (1990), 'RAF-Austeiger – Wie die Wasserfaelle', 13 August.

Deutsch, H. (1977), *Psicologia della donna* (Turin: Boringhieri).

Eco, U. (1986), 'La bustina di Minerva', *Espresso*, 5 October.

Fabricius Band, M. (1978), 'Frauen in der Isolation', in *Frauen und Terror*, ed. S. Paczensky (Hamburg: Rowohlt) pp. 58–9.

Fare, I. (1979), *Mara e le altre* (Milan: Feltrinelli).

Fedeli, L. (1982), *Mondo 3 femminile: Crisi d'identità e scienza della donna* (Rome: Bulzoni Editore).

Feinman, C. (1980), *Women in the Criminal Justice Systems* (New York: Praeger).

Fioravanti, G., 'La Notte della Repubblica', *RAIDUE*, 12 December 1989–11 April 1990.

Fornari, F. (1976), *Simbolo e Codice* (Milan: Feltrinelli).

Foucault, M. (1975), *Surveiller et punir: Naissance de la prison* (Paris: Editions Gallimard).

Franceschini, A. (1988), *Mara, Renato ed Io* (Milan: Mandadori).

Freud, A. (1967), *L'io e i meccanismi di difesa* (Florence: Martinelli).

Freud, S. (1929), *Il disagio della civiltá* in vol. 10 of *Freud Opere*, ed. L. Trilling and S. Marcus (Turin: Boringhieri).

Fromm, E. (1973), *The Anatomy of Human Destructiveness* (New York: Holt, Rinehart and Winston).

Funke, M. (1978), *Extremismus im Demokratischen Rechtsstaat* (Dusseldorf: Droste Verlag).

Galimberti, U. (1989), *Il gioco delle opinioni* (Milan: Feltrinelli).

Galmozzi, E. (1990), 'La Notte della Repubblica', *RAIDUE*, 12 December 1989–11 April 1990.

Gerhard, U. (1993), 'Women's Experiences of Injustice: Some Methodological Problems and Empirical Findings of Legal Research', *Social and Legal Studies*, **2**, pp. 303–21.

Giani Gallino, T. (1986), *La ferita e il re* (Milan: Cortina).

Gilligan, C. (1982), *In a Different Voice* (Cambridge, Mass.: Harvard University Press).

Guerra, P. (1988), 'Testimonianze', in P. Guerra (ed.), *Rivista di Storia Contemporanea* (Turin: Loescher Editore) pp. 255–80.

Guicciardi, L. (1988), *Il tempo del furore* (Milan: Rusconi).

Gulotta, G. (ed.) (1987), *Trattato di psicologia giudiziaria nel sistema penale* (Milan: Giuffrè Editore).

Hamman, A. B. (1914) 'Professor Beyer and the Woman Question', *Educational Review*, **47**, p. 296.

Hecht-Schafran, L. (1995), 'Overwhelming Evidence: Gender Bias in the Courts', in R. B. Price and N. Solokoff (eds), *The Criminal Justice System and Women* (London: McGraw-Hill).

Heidenson, F. (1968), 'The Deviance of Women: a Critique and an Enquiry', *British Journal of Sociology*, **19**, p. 2.

168   *References*

Home Office (1983), *Criminal Statistics: England and Wales, 1982* (London: HMSO), p. 29.

Jacobs, M. (1978), 'Civil Rights and Women's Rights in the Federal Republic of Germany Today', *New German Critique*, **13**.

Jacques, E. (1978), *Lavoro, creatività e giustizia sociale* (Turin: Boringhieri).

Kanisza, G. (1980), *Grammatica del vedere* (Bologna: Il Mulino).

Kaplan, G. (1992), *Contemporary Western European Feminism* (Sydney: Allen & Unwin).

Korte-Pucklitsch, I. (1978), 'Warum werden Frauen Terroristen', *Merkur*, **2**.

Koyalskaja, E., Ljubatovic, O. and Zasulich, V. (1979), *Memorie di donne terroriste* (Rome: Savelli Editore).

Krech, D., Crutchfield, R. and Ballachey, E., (1962) *Individuals in Society: Textbook of Social Psychology* (New York: McGraw-Hill).

Kutchinsky, B. (1973), 'The Legal Consciousness: a Survey of Research on Knowledge and Opinion about Law', in *Knowledge and Opinion about Law*, ed. A. Podgorecki, W. Kaupan and W. Van Houtte (London: Robertson).

Lombroso, C. (1903), *La donna delinquente* (Turin: Bocca) [English translation: *The Female Offender*, New York: Appleton, 1920].

Lombroso, C. and Ferrero, W. (1923) *La donna delinquente, la prostituta e la donna normale* (Turin: Bocca).

McLeod, E. (1982), *Women Working: Prostitution Now* (London: Croom Helm).

Maggiolini, A. (1988), *La teoria dei codici affettivi di F. Fornari* (Milan: Edizioni Unicopli).

Malagutti, G. (1987/1988), 'Delinquenza femminile comune e politica', specialisation thesis in clinical criminology, unpublished (Milan: Università degli Studi).

Mannheim, H. (1965), *Comparative Criminology* (London: Routledge & Kegan Paul).

Mathieu, V. (1972), *La speranza nella rivoluzione* (Milan: Rizzoli).

Mitscherlich-Nielsen, M. (1978), 'Hexen oder Maertyrer?', in *Frauen und terror*, ed. S. Paczensky (Hamburg: Rowohlt) p. 27.

Novelli, D. T. (1988), *Vite sospese: Le generazioni del terrorismo* (Milan: Garzanti).

Oekinghaus, E. (1925), *Die gesellschaftliche und rechtliche Stellung der deutschen Frau* (Jena: Fischer).

Passerini, L. (1988), 'Ferite della memoria: Immaginario e ideologia in una storia recente', in *Rivista di Storia Contemporanea*, ed. P. Guerra (Turin: Loescher Editore) pp. 183–255.

Petersen, H. (1992), 'On Women and Legal Concepts: Informal Law and the Norm of Consideration', *Social and Legal Studies*, **1**, pp. 493–513.

Picard, R. G. and Adams, P. D. (1987), 'Characterizations of Acts and Perpetrators of Political Violence in Three Elite U.S. Daily Newspapers', in Alali, A. O. and Eke, K. K. (eds), *Media Coverage of Terrorism* (Sage, 1991).

Pike, L. O. (1876), *History of Crime in England* (London: Smith & Elder).

Pitch, T. (1992), 'A Sexual Difference Approach to the Criminal Question', *Social and Legal Studies*, **1**, pp. 357–67.

Pollak, O. (1961), *The Criminality of Women* (New York: A. S. Barnes).

Price, R. B. and Solokoff, N. J. (eds) (1995), *The Criminal Justice System and Women* (McGraw-Hill).

Rowbotham, S. (1974), *Hidden from History* (Pluto Press, 1974).

Schmid, A. P. and de Graaf, J. (1982), *Violence as Communication* (London: Sage).

Schmid, A. P. and Jongman, A. J. (1988), *Political Terrorism*, rev. edn (New York: North-Holland).

Soro, G. (1991), *Il soggetto senza origine* (Milan: Raffaello Cortina).

Spataro, A. (1982), *Requisitoria introduttiva al processo Tobagi*, unpublished. (Milan: La Procura della Repubblica).

Swap, W. C. (ed.) (1984), *Group Decision Making* (London: Sage).

Thomas, W. I. (1923), *The Unadjusted Girl* (New York: Harper & Row).

Thuermer-Rohr, C. (1978), 'Erfahrungen mir Gewalt', in *Freuen und Terror*, ed. S. Paczensky (Hamburg: Rowohlt) p. 95.

Tololyan, K. (1989), *Narrative Culture and the Motivation of the Terrorist* (London: Sage Publications).

Weiss, J. G. (1976), 'Liberation and Crime, the Invention of the New Female Criminality', *Crime and Social Justice*, **6**: p. 17.

Wilkinson, P. (1974), *Political Terrorism* (London,: Macmillan).

Winnicott, D. W. (1986), *Home Is Where We Start From* (London: Penguin Books).

Zasulic, Y., Ljubatovic, O. and Koyalskaja, E. (1979), *Memorie di donne terroriste* (Rome: Savelli Editore).

Index